FOUL DEEDS & SUSPICIOUS DEATHS
IN AND AROUND BARNSLEY

Foul Deeds and Suspicious Deaths in and Around

BARNSLEY

Geoffrey Howse

Wharncliffe Books

This book is dedicated to my Mother,
Doreen for her unfailing support

First published in Great Britain in 2007 by
Wharncliffe Books
an imprint of
Pen & Sword Books Ltd
47 Church Street
Barnsley
South Yorkshire
S70 2AS

© Geoffrey Howse 2007

ISBN: 978 184563 032 4

Typeset in Plantin and ITC Benguiat by
Mousemat Design Limited

Printed and bound in Great Britain by CPI UK

Pen & Sword Books Ltd incorporates the imprints of
Pen & Sword Aviation, Pen & Sword Maritime,
Pen & Sword Military, Wharncliffe Local History,
Pen and Sword Select, Pen and Sword Military Classics
and Leo Cooper.

For a complete list of Pen & Sword titles please contact
PEN & SWORD BOOKS LIMITED
47 Church Street, Barnsley, South Yorkshire,
S70 2AS, England
E-mail: enquiries@pen-and-sword.co.uk
Website: www.pen-and-sword.co.uk

Contents

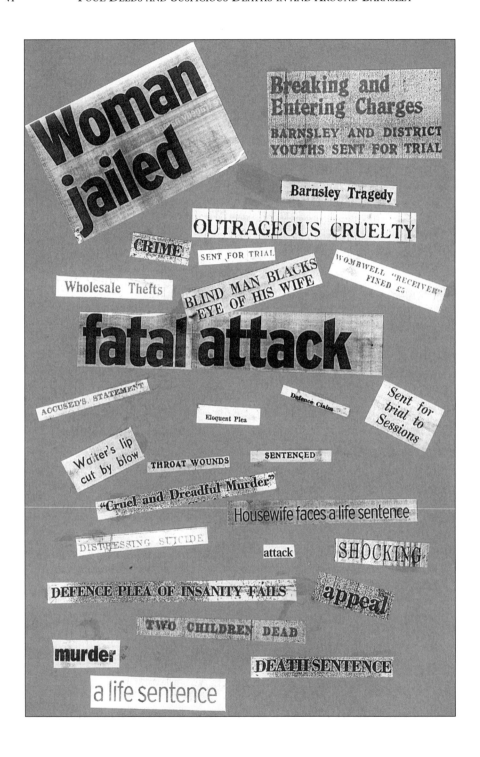

Introduction

True crime and foul and sinister goings-on seem to make fascinating reading to a large number of people. Despite the often horrific content of some accounts, particularly involving murder, the public is ever thirsty for more and more gruesome details of what man is capable of doing to his fellow man, or indeed to the animals in his charge. This is my fifth book involving true crime. My first four featured crimes, mostly murders, committed in London. This is my first book involving crimes perpetrated around the area where I grew up.

Sometimes a particular crime sticks in one's mind above all others for one reason or another. Growing up as I did, firstly in Elsecar and afterwards in Hoyland, then as now at the epicentre of important historical events and surrounded by magnificent countryside of unsurpassed beauty for many a mile around, I was sheltered from some of the more sensational crimes of the late 1950s and 1960s that took place during my formative years. We had television of course but my family didn't spend an inordinately long time viewing because there was always something else far more interesting to do. The occasional cartoon, film, variety show, nature programme, important royal or national event was our preferred choice and my father would tune in to watch the racing, wrestling and football results on Saturday afternoons if he wasn't off angling somewhere. Sometimes I watched the news but didn't take much notice of events that seemed so far removed from the goings on in my own locality. Crime, particularly murder, was confined to the odd gangster film (I remember Edward G Robinson and James Cagney being firm favourites) or the early James Bond films I managed to get to see at Elsecar's Futurist cinema.

Apart from vague recollections of hearing about the Kennedy assassination in 1963, the first real murders I can remember being aware of were the Moors Murders of 1965, and I think that was because they involved children, and the names of Hindley and Brady were on everyone's lips. I can also remember the Braybrook Street Massacre the following year.

From an early age I was an avid reader but my reading rarely extended to the columns of our daily newspaper, the Daily Mail, or indeed the local weekly journals, which my mother read with great interest.

It was to be the murder of a local girl in 1972 that eventually grabbed my attention, and which subsequently encouraged me to take an interest in crime and the darker side of human existence. Since that time both the name and the image of the unfortunate victim, a strikingly pretty, fourteen-year-old schoolgirl, has remained imprinted on my mind. She lived less than two miles from my own home in Hoyland and the tragic circumstances surrounding her rape and murder rocked not just Barnsley and district but appalled the sensibilities of the entire nation. Researching the case of Shirley Boldy, that unfortunate victim of rape and murder, brought memories flooding back of the closing years of my schooldays. A more recent case included here involves one of my fellow classmates at Kirk Balk School. She murdered her husband and it certainly sends a chill down one's spine when one is writing about a person one knows or knew. Indeed, a short while ago in my book *The A to Z of London Murders* I had occasion to write about the savage and as yet still unsolved murder of a personal friend. I did not find it an easy task.

Writing about the long dead is not nearly so harrowing as when writing about more recent cases. I have tried to deal sensitively with the subjects I have chosen and, in some cases I have written about highly emotive events which can be deeply upsetting to the relatives of victims of crime or indeed the relatives of the criminals, or those affected by the perpetrators of the many foul deeds included here. Ultimately these cases are a matter of record and I have drawn from many sources in order to present as true an account as possible. I apologise unreservedly for any omissions or errors.

It is perhaps a little insensitive to say that Barnsley and the surrounding area has a rich history of crime. When one writes or talks about something having a rich history one is not as a rule thinking about the darker side of existence. Nevertheless the fact remains that since greater documentary evidence exists from the closing years of the eighteenth century and throughout the nineteenth and twentieth century right up to the present day, it is apparent that there has been a considerable number of killings and serious crimes committed throughout the area; those I have been able to include here are quite literally the tip of the iceberg. I have selected a cross section of serious crimes

Central Barnsley c. *1935.* Author's collection

and foul deeds, some seemingly petty incidents, others more quirky, in order to give the reader a varied sample of Barnsley and district's darker past.

Suicide, was once regarded as a criminal offence and failed suicides were often hanged afterwards. In Acts of Parliament passed in 1879 and 1882 suicide ceased to be regarded as a homicide but it was not until 1961 that suicide was finally decriminalised.

During my research into the various subjects featured within these pages I have come across a wide range of killings, and a whole array of foul deeds. There have been occasions when I have found it difficult to decide exactly where the foul deed lies, whether it really lies with the perpetrator of the crime or misdemeanour or indeed, whether it lies with those sitting in judgement who dished out a disproportionately harsh sentence. I will leave it for the reader to decide. Occasionally when one is working on a book information comes from a surprising source. A retired journalist contacted me during the time I was writing the Green Linnet chapter, concerning some of my published books about Hoyland and district. We had a lengthy conversation and it turned out this octogenarian gentleman worked on some Yorkshire newspapers during his early career and later for

The Times. During the 1950s he would often come home late at night to the family home in Wombwell. The Yorkshire Traction Company were the principal omnibus operators at that time but the Wombwell firm of T Burrows and Son ran a later service from Barnsley to Wombwell. He used to catch that last bus home and remembers Clara Farrell (see Chapter 11), the 'Green Linnet', as she was known, always being on it, presumably after plying her trade in Barnsley. She habitually got off the bus in Wombwell at the stop before he did. He also remembers there being another prostitute working in Barnsley during that same period, known as the 'Black Swan'.

During my last few weeks of research into crime in Barnsley I came across so many interesting and sometimes sensational cases, often involving murder, which I have been unable to include here but which has indicated that there is a veritable feast of subject matter to tap into, and in the not too distant future there could be at least one more book on foul deeds and suspicious deaths in and around Barnsley.

Acknowledgements

Iris Ackroyd, Keith Atack, Vera Atack, Michael Barber, Susan Barber, Joan Bostwick, Norma Braddick, Robert (Bob) Alan Dale, Kathleen Dale, Iris J Deller, Joanna C Murray Deller, Ricky S Deller, Tracy P Deller, Brian Elliott, Ian Harley, Janet Hinchcliffe, Ann Howse, Kathleen Howse, Dr Hidayat Hussein, Brendan E McNally, Raymond Mellor-Jones, Eleanor Nelder, Stanley Nelder, Anthony Richards, Chris Sharp of Old Barnsley, Helen Vodden, Adam R Walker, Anna Walker, Christine & David Walker of Walkers' Newsagents at Hoyland, Darren J Walker, Emma C Walker, Ivan P Walker, Paula L Walker, Suki B Walker, Clifford Willoughby, Margaret Willoughby, Kate Ward, the staff of Barnsley Central Library Local Studies, the staff of the British Library Newspaper Archive, Colindale; and I would particularly like to thank John D Murray who has assisted me over many years.

CHAPTER 1

An Assortment of Crimes and Foul Deeds in Barnsley and District 1854–1995

BIGAMY AT WORSBROUGH, 1854
...she knew he was already married.

On Wednesday 11 June 1855, James Dalton appeared at the Yorkshire Summer Assizes at York before Mr Justice Crowder, charged with bigamy. The Hon Mr Wortley prosecuted. The court heard that on 20 May 1844 the prisoner had married Mary Rawbottom at Wigan in Lancashire. Then, on 22 April 1854, he married Maria Davies at Worsbrough, his wife Mary at that time and on the day of the trial, still being alive. Dalton's defence brought into question the fidelity of his first wife and it

The village of Worsbrough with St Mary's Church at its heart. Chris Sharp of Old Barnsley

was established that she and he had mutually agreed to separate. On being found guilty of the charge the judge explained the leniency of the sentence – one month's imprisonment. This was because Dalton's second wife had not been deceived, as she knew he was already married.

❧

ASSAULT AND ROBBERY AT WORSBROUGH, 1854
...assaulted and robbed William Robinson of a watch and other articles...

On Wednesday 5 December 1854, Amos Mellor, aged twenty-four, of Worsbrough, appeared at York Assizes before Mr Justice Crowder. He was indicted for having assaulted and robbed William Robinson of a watch and other articles at Worsbrough on 12 November. Found guilty, he was sentenced to six years penal servitude.

❧

VIOLENT ASSAULT BY FURNACEMEN AT HOYLAND, APRIL 1855
...he was attacked by the three men without provocation and severely beaten.

On Friday and Saturday 1 and 2 June 1855, William Walker was the presiding judge at the monthly courts held at Barnsley Court House. On Friday, one of the first cases to be heard was that of Luke Walton *v* Robert Hodgson, Edward Ward and Benjamin Gadd. All four men were residents of Kitroyd, Hoyland and all were in the employ of Messrs Dawes at Milton Ironworks - as furnacemen. Mr Tyas appeared for Mr Walton, the plaintiff and Mr Hamer for the defendants. The action was brought to recover £8 damages for an assault that took place on 8 April. On that day, as Mr Walton was returning home from work he was - according to one person's testimony - attacked by the three men without provocation and severely beaten. It was Hodgson who actually inflicted the blows while his co-defendants egged him on. Robert Hodgson said that on the night of 1 April he had been in the company of Luke Walton and that Walton had called him 'rotten', afterwards saying he was 'not a man, and could soon break him to pieces'. In his efforts to prove that Walton was the actually aggressor, Hodgson failed. The judge expressed that although Walton was not entirely free from blame, the defendant Walton was the worst of the pair and ought to pay some damages. In passing judgement against Hodgson, he discharged Ward and Gadd. Hodgson was ordered to pay £5 damages and costs amounting to twenty-five shillings. He was further ordered to pay these in instalments of £1 per month.

ॐ

STABBING AT GAWBER, MAY 1955
They have run something into me.

On Wednesday 6 June 1855, Thomas Turner of Gawber and a boy named William White appeared at Barnsley Court House before G Wentworth, T Taylor, V Corbett and the Rev W Wordsworth, charged with a serious assault upon Mr T Fieldsend of Higham on Saturday 19 May. On that day Mr Fieldsend had been in Barnsley and began his return journey home at nightfall. He was overtaken by Thomas Turner and some other men near Jordan Hill when, without any particular reason, declared that he wished to fight Mr Fieldsend. The latter, having no wish to fight declined and continued his journey home. A while later Mr Fieldsend arrived at Gawber

Gawber Hall, near where Mr T Fieldsend was stabbed in 1855. Chris Sharp of Old Barnsley

Hall, where several men were gathered near a corner. As he passed by some stones were thrown at him. Once again Turner stepped forward from the group and said to Fieldsend:

Thou art bound to fight here.

Mr Fieldsend once again refused but within moments was heard to call out:

They have run something into me.

The court was shown Mr Fieldsend's bloodstained trousers and a stocking saturated with blood. Dr Jackson testified as to the serious nature of Mr Fieldsend's injuries. The Bench inflicted a penalty of £5 on Turner and White or the option to spend two months in Wakefield Gaol.

~~~

ASSAULT ON AN APPRENTICE, BARNSLEY, 1856
Mr Senior came over and struck him on both sides of the head with his hands.

Cabinetmaker Charles Senior of Graham's Orchard, Barnsley, appeared before magistrates at Barnsley Court House on Wednesday 5 March 1856, charged with assaulting his apprentice, William Umpleby, on 26 February. Mr Tyas appeared for the complainant and Mr Hamer for the defendant. William Umpleby said he entered service as an apprentice with Mr Senior in October 1854. For the first year, during which time he was to receive no wages, all went well. However, since October 1855, when he had begun to receive a wage, Mr Senior's ill-treatment of him had commenced. On 26 February another boy asked Umpleby to help him move a sofa, which he refused to do, having already been given a task requiring his more immediate attention. However, on hearing Umpleby's refusal to help the boy, Mr Senior came over and struck him on both sides of the head with his hands. Mr Hamer argued that as his employer Mr Senior had a right to chastise his apprentice if he had done wrong. When the agreement between Charles Senior and William Umpleby was examined it was discovered to have been drawn up on paper with a half-crown stamp, and not properly formalised. No damages were awarded but Charles Senior, was ordered to pay 7s 6d costs.

THE WOMBWELL STABBING CASE, 1860

...I found a wound in his left temple, three inches in length, cut down to the bone.

On Monday 9 July 1860, Nathanial Alsopp, a miner, who was employed at Wombwell Main found himself in the dock at Barnsley Court House, before Thomas Taylor, Esq, and Colonel Daly. Alsopp was charged with cutting and wounding Thomas Whalley, at Wombwell, on the night of 30 June. The delay in hearing the case was in consequence of the prosecutor, Thomas Whalley being unable to attend and give evidence, as a result of him not having until that time, sufficiently recovered from the injuries inflicted upon him by Alsopp. In his evidence Whalley told the court that he was a collier and worked in the same pit as the defendant, Alsopp. It transpired that on Saturday 30 June he was with Alsopp and others at the *Horseshoes* public house, Wombwell, and they all left together after their drinking session, at about twelve o'clock.

The men resided about a mile from the *Horseshoes*. After they had walked a distance of about a quarter of a mile Whalley said to Alsopp that he thought he was a shabby fellow for calling for

Wombwell Main, where Nathanial Alsopp was employed. Chris Sharp of Old Barnsley

a quart of ale and not paying for it. Alsopp's response was to call Whalley 'a fucking rogue', to which Whalley replied that if he repeated the words again he would give him a smack in the mouth. A fight then broke out between the two men and it lasted for several rounds, although no indication was given as to exactly how long this impromptu fight actually lasted. During the last round Whalley said that he discovered he had been stabbed in several places. He called out: 'I have been stabbed' at which point Alsopp promptly took to his heels and fled the scene. Whalley's evidence was corroborated in every detail by John Gaffney, collier, one of the party who had left the *Horseshoes* with Whalley and Alsopp. Gaffney added that when Whalley complained of having being stabbed, Alsopp said: 'I think the bastard has got enough, I don't think he will come again.' He also gave evidence that he did not see the prisoner have anything in his hand. However, William Wison, a collier, stated that he saw the prisoner put his right hand into his trouser pocket, and take out something, although he had been unable to see exactly what it was.

When Police Constable John Bridgett arrested Alsopp, the prisoner denied all knowledge of having stabbed Whalley.

The Horseshoes, *Wombwell, where Nathanial Alsopp was drinking with Thomas Whalley on Monday 9 July 1860.* Chris Sharp of Old Barnsley

However, there were bloodstains on his clothes. Whalley's own clothes, saturated with blood, were also shown in evidence. Mr J R L Hallett gave evidence to the nature of the injuries received by Whalley. He told the court:

> *I am a surgeon at Hoyland Nether. On Sunday morning, the 1st July, I was called upon to go to Wombwell Main. I went and saw the prosecutor. I found a wound in his left temple, three inches in length, cut down to the bone. A cut on the outer corner of the left eyebrow. Another from the middle of the ear, entering into the cheek, two and a half inches in length. A slight cut in the neck. Another on the left corner of the upper lip penetrating into the mouth. Another cut or stab two inches below the left arm pit. The wounds, eight in number, were not of a dangerous character. The patient was in a very low condition from loss of blood.*

The prisoner, who appeared greatly affected by the evidence given, said that it was all owing to getting too much liquor, or it would never have happened. Alsopp told the court that he had a wife and children in Lancashire, and they would be 'clamming' (starving) in consequence of his being locked up. He said that he had never until this time in his life appeared before a magistrate, and would take care that he never was before one again. He added that he would give up drinking from that time.

It was reported in the *Barnsley Chronicle* that Mr Taylor addressed the prisoner in 'a most feeling manner in the nature of his offence and the evil effects of intoxication'. He told Alsopp that he and his brother magistrate, having taken all the circumstances into considerations had decided to treat the case as one of common assault. Alsopp was fined £5.00 or in default, two months hard labour. The prisoner told the court that he had £2 2s. owing to him in wages, and he thought he could raise the remainder if they gave him time. Alsopp was then removed to the lock-up.

❦

ASSAULT AT HOYLAND NETHER, 1860
...she had thrown a basin into the defendant's house, and a poker at her door.

When Elizabeth Smith of Hoyland brought a charge of assault against her neighbour, Jane Banks, in September 1860, the outcome of the hearing held at Barnsley Court House was not what the prosecutor had expected. Magistrate Thomas Taylor Esq listened to the evidence placed before him. He was informed that the two women had for some time lived at variance with each other and that on the previous Friday matters came to a head, in consequence of something that was said. The two women came to blows, the defendant, Banks, striking the complainant, Smith, over the back and arm with a poker, inflicting a severe injury. During the course of the evidence placed before the court the complainant admitted that in the lead up to these events, she had thrown a basin into the defendant's house, and a poker at her door. After a few moments of deliberation with his colleagues, the chairman said that as the complainant was the first to use the poker, she must pay the expenses of bringing the case before the court, which amounted to 15s. 6d. No further action was taken in respect of the assault.

***

SAVED BY HIS ELOQUENCE, ELSECAR, 1860
...prisoner pleaded a perfect state of non-responsibility and obliviousness...

On the evening of Sunday 16 September 1860, James Taylor found himself in police custody charged with 'pocketing' two half-pint drinking glasses and a 'mug', the property of Edwin

A Victorian view looking up Stubbin (now Hill Street), Elsecar. Author's collection

Pepper, proprietor of the *Stubbin Hotel*, Elsecar. When he appeared at Barnsley Court House the following week, his eloquence and earnestness must have raised a wry smile or two. The prisoner pleaded a perfect state of non-responsibility and obliviousness, through having permitted too easy an access to his mouth of an enemy who 'stole away his brains', in the temporary absence of which he himself became an unwilling purloiner of the articles mentioned. Presumably as a result of Mr Taylor's eloquence, and perhaps after reflecting on matters concerning the provision of the said 'enemy' for ready money to the defendant by himself, Mr Pepper did not press the charges, and the prisoner was discharged with a severe reprimand from the magistrates. Taylor was also warned that if he ever committed himself in the same way again it might be worse for him. On paying the court's expenses he was discharged.

☙❧

SMALL FINE FOR ASSAULT ON A CONSTABLE AT HOYLE MILL, 1862
...assault on Police Constable Coates, at Ridsdale's public-house...

In February 1862, James Walker was fined one shilling and costs, for an assault on Police Constable Coates, at *Ridsdale's* public house, Hoyle Mill. His fellow reveller, James Airstone, charged with aiding and abetting was discharged. The smallness of the fine was in consequence of Constable Coates having 'laid open' Walker's head with his truncheon.

☙❧

WOMAN REPRIMANDED FOR STEALING FROM THE WORKHOUSE AT BARNSLEY, 1862
...for leaving her children destitute in the Sheffield Road.

On Monday 10 February 1862, Mary Rushforth appeared before Thomas Taylor, Esq at Barnsley Court House. Mary Rushforth, who had at various times been an inmate of the workhouse, was charged with taking away clothes belonging to the Union. On the night of Friday 7 February she left the workhouse with the clothes in her possession. She, having two children in the workhouse, returned the following morning minus the clothes she had taken. Police Superintendent Greenhalgh told the court that the woman had previously been

An Edwardian view of Sheffield Road, Barnsley, showing the mostly early and mid-nineteenth century buildings which would have been familiar to Mary Rushforth. Chris Sharp of Old Barnsley

before the magistrates for leaving her children destitute in the Sheffield Road. Mr Taylor gave Mary Rushforth a severe reprimand and told her if she repeated the offence she would be sent to the House of Correction at Wakefield.

***

PERSISTENT OFFENDER GIVEN OPTION, 1862
...obtaining goods by false pretences...

On Wednesday 26 February 1862, Emma Winter, a persistent offender, appeared at Barnsley Court House and pleaded guilty to pawning a gown to the value of twelve shillings, the property of Emma Beevers. Police Superintendent Greenhalgh told the court that there were several charges against her for obtaining goods by false pretences, but these were not gone into. The bench ordered her to pay a fine of twenty shillings, or in default, to be imprisoned in the House of Correction for one month.

STARVING WIFE DEPRIVED OF HUSBAND, 1862
... in consequence of his wife being in a state of actual starvation.

During the last week of February 1862, William Manning of Barnsley appeared before Thomas Taylor, Esq at Barnsley Court House, charged with stealing a brass tap and some lead piping from the premises of Mr T Cordeux, in Pitt Street, on 20 February. Manning pleaded guilty to the offence and in mitigation said he had been actuated to commit the felony in consequence of his wife being in a state of starvation. He was sentenced to three months imprisonment at Wakefield, with hard labour, under the Vagrancy Act.

❧

ASSAULTS ON POLICE IN JUNE 1864
...he found a fellow constable was being kicked and beaten upon the floor by several men...

A powerful looking fellow named Henry Rusby appeared in the dock at Barnsley Court House on Wednesday 30 June 1864, charged with assaulting Police Constable Robinson at Green Moor on 4 June. Police Constable Robinson, having been ill for some time, had only returned to duty on the day the assault against him took place. On the day in question Police Constable Robinson was on foot patrol and, observing a large number of people behaving in a disorderly manner outside a public house at Green Moor, walked up to them and requested that they disperse and retire peaceably to their houses. This they did. As Police Constable Robinson walked away, the prisoner in the dock, Rusby, called out to him:

Here policeman. I want to speak to you.

The officer went up to Rusby, who immediately knocked him down, pulled his hair and screwed his thumb so violently as to dislocate it. A boy named Fieldsend, living at Crane Moor, gave evidence that he had overheard a conversation between Rusby and another man, shortly before the assault took place, in which Rusby said that he would 'like to kick the policeman'. Rusby was found guilty of assault and fined twenty shillings, or in default to be imprisoned for one month.

Also on 30 June 1864, at Barnsley Court House, William

Flowers and William Hill appeared in the dock charged with assaulting Police Sergeant Branagan on 21 June. The officer was on duty in Wilson Street on the day in question, when hearing a great disturbance at the *Freedom Inn*, he went there, and after entering the premises he was attracted to one of the rooms in which a violent dispute appeared to be going on. On entering the room he found a fellow constable was being kicked and beaten upon the floor by several men, among whom were Flowers and Hill. When Sergeant Branagan went to the constable's aid he was assaulted by Flowers and Hill. Flowers and Hill denied the charge from the dock, and suggested it was the police officers who were to blame as they were drunk when they entered the *Freedom Inn*. The Bench, however, did not attach much credit to the prisoners' version of events and fined each of them twenty shillings and costs, or one month imprisonment in default.

Also at the same hearing, Robert Pinder, a labourer at the Elsecar ironworks, was charged with having, on 22 June, at Hoyland Nether, assaulted Police Constable Jones, into whose custody he had been given for breaking, whilst in a state of intoxication, a quantity of crockery belonging to a hawker. He was given a fine of five shillings and ordered to pay costs.

☙☙☙

SUSPICION OF ARSON BY AN UNSATISFACTORY MAID, 1864
... there was great suspicion attached to Miss Woodward's conduct.

On Monday 4 July 1864, a respectably dressed young lady came up before Thomas Taylor, Esq at Barnsley Court House. Ann Woodward was charged with having set fire to a quantity of clothing and furniture in an upper room of the living quarters at the *Vine Tavern*, Pitt Street, Barnsley, on 1 July. Her employer, Mrs Coward had engaged the girl a little over six weeks previously. However, after a fortnight, Miss Woodward having proved so unsatisfactory in carrying out her duties, had been given a month's notice to leave. That notice had expired on the Friday that the fire occurred. Woodward left the *Vine Tavern* at about ten o'clock in the evening, taking what remained of her belongings with her. About ten minutes later Mrs Coward went upstairs and was alarmed to see flames coming from a closet through which Woodward would have passed on the way to and from her bedroom. She raised the alarm and with assistance was able to extinguish the flames. Luckily, although not without considerable difficulty, a box containing the clothes of the girl who had been engaged to replace Woodward, was saved from the flames. Mrs Coward told the court that she was certain that Ann Woodward was the last person upstairs before the fire broke out. Woodward said that she took a candle upstairs on Friday night, but the candle went out. She relighted it with matches which she threw upon the closet floor, thinking they were out. Mr Taylor having considered the evidence concluded that there was great suspicion attached to Miss Woodward's conduct. He sentenced her to twenty-four hours imprisonment with bread and water.

∽∼∾

DETERMINED ASSAULT AT THE
WELLINGTON INN, 1864
...*suspiciously pugnacious-looking young fellows*...

On 9 July 1864, the *Barnsley Chronicle* included a report of the proceedings at Barnsley Court House on Wednesday 6 July, before T E Taylor, Esq in which it recorded:

Three suspiciously pugnacious-looking young fellows, named James Sellars, James Siddons and Alfred Holling, were charged with assaulting another member of their fraternity, named James Jagger, in the Wellington Inn, *Barnsley, on the night of Saturday last...*

On the night of Saturday 2 July, James Jagger was seated in the *Wellington Inn* when Sellars, Siddons and Hollings entered the bar. Sellars and Holling went over to Jagger and struck him then kicked him, egged on by Siddons. The landlord ejected Sellars, Siddons and Holling, then sent for a policeman, who accompanied James Jagger home. The assault being corroborated by Mr Nixon, Mr Taylor fined the three men 1*s*. each and costs.

∽∼∾

MAN ACQUITTED OF ATTEMPTED MURDER OF
WIFE RECEIVES LONG SENTENCE FOR SERIOUS
ASSAULT, BARNSLEY, 1868
She was insensible and bleeding from the lips and chin...

On Monday 28 December 1868, labourer Peter Porter appeared in the dock at Barnsley Court House, before E Newman and F H Taylor, charged with cutting and wounding

Martha Porter, his wife, with intent to kill, on 16 December. Mrs Porter, the victim of the attack was the first witness to be called. She told the court:

> I reside in Foundry-street, in Barnsley. The prisoner, Peter Porter, is my husband. We have been married for the last twenty-six years. I have had seven children by him. We have not lived together since the month of January last. Five of my children live with me. My husband is a weaver by trade. He has occasionally come to my house, but not to stay there. A week since last Wednesday night, the 16th of December, the prisoner came to my house about half-past six o'clock. I was in along with my two little girls. My husband was sober. He came and put his face to mine, and said, 'Do you think you are doing what is right?' I said, 'Yes: I do not know that I am doing anything wrong.' He then said, 'Where were you last night?' I said 'I was at St. George's School tea-party.' He said, 'You are a liar. What time did you get home?' I said, 'About ten o'clock, as near as I can tell.' He said, 'Did you go without bonnet?' I said, 'No.' After some words he said, 'Have I not told you that I would do you your job?' I said, 'Yes, many a time.' He then up with his fist and gave me a blow on the right side of my head, and I have no recollection of anything afterwards. When I came to myself, I found I was laid upon a swab. At the time I was struck by the prisoner I had been ironing some clothes. When he came in I had the iron flat on the table. There was another iron on the fire. The irons produced are what I referred to. I have been attended by Mr Blackburn ever since. I am very ill, and not able to follow my employment. I go out as a charwoman. I was very much burnt about the thighs and the lower parts of my body.'

John Blackburn, surgeon, told the court:

> On the 16th of this month I was called upon to see Martha Porter. I found her at her own house in Foundry-street, Barnsley. She was down stairs, laid upon a long settle. She was insensible and bleeding from the lips and chin, the blood issuing from three incised wounds. The largest was on the chin and about an inch and a half long. The two other incisions were cut through the lower lip into the mouth, and about an inch-long each. She also had a severe contused wound on the right cheek bone which had closed the right eye. I should say the wound had been inflicted by a knife. I also examined her

thighs, and found that she was suffering from a severe bruise on each thigh, the left thigh mark corresponding exactly in shape to the flat side of a smoothing iron, and the right wound corresponding to the edge of a smoothing iron. I have attended her ever since, and she is now under my care and treatment, and will be for some time. I considered her at the time I first saw her in great danger.

Sarah Ann Woodiwiss, a widow, resident in Silver Street told the court that she attended to Mrs Porter before the doctor arrived but did not see Peter Porter in the house. James Porter, son of the injured woman and prisoner, who lived only a short distance from his mother's house said that on 16 December on hearing his mother's screams he rushed to her house, where he saw her laying on the floor by the side of the fire. He also said he saw his father kick his mother twice before he rushed out of the house. James Porter said he followed his father and collared him at the end of Cannon Street. He shortly let his father go and hurried to the surgeon Mr Blackburn to ask him to attend to his

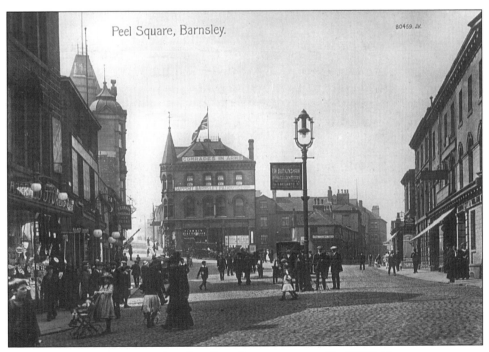

Peel Square, Barnsley, where Peter Porter was arrested by PC Haigh on 16 December 1868. Chris Sharp of Old Barnsley

mother. Later that evening Peter Porter was arrested by PC Haigh in Peel Square. On being charged with ill-using his wife, Porter said:

She has caused me to do it, but I love her.

When he was searched at the police station Porter was found to have two knives concealed in his clothes. Porter said:

I can clearly say I am not guilty of either burning or cutting. I struck her, then kicked her as she fell on the bedstock top.

Having heard the evidence the Bench committed Porter to stand trial at the next Leeds Assizes. He was refused bail.

Peter Porter was tried at Leeds Spring Assizes in April indicted for having wounded Martha Porter with intent to murder her. A second count in the indictment charged him with wounding her with intent to do her grievous bodily harm. Despite the prosecution's strong case against him the jury found him guilty on only the minor count and he was sentenced to seven years penal servitude.

⌒⌒⌒

BRUTAL ASSAULT AT JUMP, 1891
...rushed out from a hiding place and struck James Fletcher a blow on the head with a fire poker...

On Tuesday 26 October 1891, at about 7pm amongst other company at the *Flying Dutchman* in Jump, were miners William Smith, Samuel Foster and James and Thomas Fletcher. An argument broke out between Samuel Foster and James Fletcher and they went outside the inn to fight. Nothing came of it and the men went their separate ways. Foster went off with Smith and Fletcher joined his brother Thomas and, after finishing their drinks, they set off for home. As they approached the National School they saw Smith and another man. One of them called out: 'They are coming'. The Foster brothers were bombarded with stones hurled at them by William Smith and the other man. Suddenly, Samuel Foster rushed out from a hiding place and struck James Fletcher a blow on the head with a poker, which felled him to the floor, rendering him insensible. Foster and Smith then began to kick him on the head and body but as assistance came the two men fled. The other unidentified

The Flying Dutchman, *Jump, where William Smith, Samuel Foster and James and Thomas Fletcher were drinking, on Tuesday 26 October 1891.*

Keith Hopkinson collection

stone thrower had by this time already disappeared. On Wednesday 28 December, William Smith and Samuel Foster appeared in the dock at Barnsley Police Court, charged with assault, before Major Vincent and Messrs Brady and Dymond. In prosecuting the two men Mr J Carrington opened by saying that once the evidence had been tendered they would see that the assault was one of the most brutal and unprovoked that had ever been heard in that court. James Fletcher told the court that since the assault he had been unable to work. This was corroborated in a letter written by Dr Ritchie and read out by Mr Carrington. Thomas Fletcher told the court that his brother's face was discoloured and the causeway near the National School was covered with blood after Smith and Foster had finished kicking him. Although both defendants said they were sorry for what they had done, the chairman, Major Vincent, said the assault was a brutal one and committed both men to spend one month in prison.

WITHOUT VISIBLE MEANS, 1892
The men had nothing to say in their defence.

It was reported in the *Barnsley Standard* that on Wednesday 13 January 1892 three 'rough looking' men appeared in the dock at Barnsley Police Court before the Mayor (Alderman Blackburn), Mr C Harvey, Alderman Marsden and Captain Ormsby. John Smith, William Brightsmore and George Harris, described as 'strangers', were charged with having slept out without any visible means of subsistence. The three men had been found sleeping in the coke ovens at the Old Oaks Colliery, Ardsley. The men had nothing to say in their defence and were each committed to fourteen days imprisonment.

∽∼∾

A DISGRACE TO HER SEX, 1892
...wept bitterly throughout the hearing...

Elizabeth Osborne appeared at Barnsley Police Court before Mr C Brady and Mr T Dymond on Monday 15 February, charged with having behaved improperly in Shambles Street on the night of Saturday 13 February. The case was proven by police constables Raven and Cunningham. It transpired that Elizabeth Osborne, described in the *Barnsley Standard* as a 'middle-aged' woman and her case highlighted under the heading 'A DISGRACE TO HER SEX', had been sent to prison many times for similar offences. She wept bitterly throughout the hearing and begged not to be sent to prison and asked the magistrates to give her a chance. Instead they committed her to serve three months with hard labour.

∽∼∾

LOOSE WOMAN BREAKS WINDOW PANES IN POLICE CELL, 1892
...appeared in the dock with a black eye.

On Monday 22 February 1892, Margaret Turner, described as a woman of ill-repute, appeared at Barnsley Police Court before Mr J Dyson and T Dymond. She was charged with having acted in a disorderly manner in Wilson Street on Sunday night. The case was proven by Police Sergeant Collins and Constable East. In addition to the first charge another was added, she having broken five panes of glass in the police cell. She was given two months for the first offence and an additional twenty-eight days for the second. The defendant appeared in the dock with a black eye. She had been convicted at Barnsley on twenty-one separate occasions. On leaving the dock after sentencing Turner commented:

You call this a Court of Justice? They'll swear any mortal thing.

༝ᢙᢙ

UNGRATEFUL LABOURER DOES DAMAGE AT WORKHOUSE, PENISTONE, 1907
...picked up a hammer and in a rage smashed a cell door...

John Kelly, a labourer of no fixed abode applied for a night's lodgings at Penistone Workhouse on Wednesday 20 March 1907. On Thursday morning having refused to undertake the requisite task work he was told he would not be allowed to leave until he had carried out the work. Kelly picked up a hammer and in a rage smashed a cell door causing 8*s*. worth of damage. He was arrested and on Friday appeared before magistrates at Barnsley Borough Court and was sent to prison for one month.

༝ᢙᢙ

THEFT FROM NEW STREET SHOP FRONT, BARNSLEY, 1908
Police Constable Shotbolt was on patrol in the vicinity when he saw a man behaving suspiciously.

At about 9.00am on Friday 31 January 1908 Arthur C Quest, pawnbroker's assistant at Messrs John Guest and Sons, New

New Street Barnsley during the Edwardian period. John Guest and Sons, where William Clarke stole some boots can be seen in the right foreground. Chris Sharp of Old Barnsley

Street, Barnsley, placed a pair of boots valued at 6s. 6d. on a shelf on the outside display. An hour later the boots were missing. Police Constable Shotbolt was on patrol in the vicinity when he saw a man behaving suspiciously. He arrested him and the boots were found hidden beneath his coat. The man concerned was William Clarke, a labourer of no fixed abode. He had recently been convicted of stealing. Clarke appeared before magistrates at Barnsley Borough Court on Friday 7 February and was sent to prison for one month.

܁܁܁

ASSAULT ON MARRIED WOMAN BY TWO SPINSTERS, HOYLE MILL, 1910
... knocked her down and blacked both her eyes.

On Friday 15 April 1910, two sisters, both spinsters, found themselves in the dock at Barnsley West Riding Court before Messrs T Norton (presiding), W A Darnford, C A Markham and J Robinson. Sarah Ann Dunn and Edith Dunn of Hoyle Mill were summoned for having assaulted Mary Ann Dodman, also of Hoyle Mill, on Wednesday 7 April. The court heard that on that day Mrs Dodman had been annoyed by some boys (including a brother of the defendants) playing football in the yard. When she remonstrated with them about it Sarah Dunn struck her, knocked her down and blacked both her eyes. Edith

Hoyle Mill, where the assault on Mrs Mary Ann Dodman took place on Wednesday 7 April 1910. Chris Sharp of Old Barnsley

Dunn also struck Mrs Dodman on the side of the head. Both women then pulled Mrs Dodman's hair. The events were corroborated in court by Mrs Dodman's husband and a twelve-year-old boy named Horace Rowley. Police Constable Wright told the court that he had received complaints from Mrs Dodman about boys playing football. The Dunn sisters were represented by Mr John Rideal of Messrs Rideal and Son. Mr Rideal in defence of his clients said that Sarah Dunn struck back at Mr Dodman when he hit her, but that she did not assault Mrs Dodman. Edith Dunn said she tried to separate her sister and Mr and Mrs Dodman when they were scuffling together. She further alleged that Mr Dodman struck his own wife and pulled her into the house by the hair of her head. This evidence was corroborated by Mrs Dunn (the defendant's mother) and two boys, Wilfred Parkin and Alfred Dunn. The bench did hot believe them and were of the opinion that an assault had been committed and fined the Dunn sisters 5*s*. each and costs.

⌒⌒⌒

INHUMAN PARENTS SENT TO PRISON, BARNSLEY, 1915
He weighed only seven pounds instead of the fourteen pounds he should have weighed normally.

On Wednesday 1 September 1915, an inquest was held at Barnsley Town Hall on the body of eight-month-old John Henderson Summons, the illegitimate child of bricklayer's labourer, James Henderson and Laura Summons, of 21 Cooper Street, Barnsley. The evidence moved the coroner, Mr P P Maitland to remark that the parents ought to be locked up and he hoped they would be punished. However, the matter might be left in the hands of the NSPCC, said Mr Maitland.

Inspector Chappell of the NSPCC stated that he had repeatedly warned Henderson and Summons to give better attention to the deceased baby. The jury returned a verdict that 'John Henderson Summons died from tubercular meningitis, following tubercular peritonitis, caused or accelerated by the very grave neglect on the part of the mother and father he was living with.'

After being severely censured by the coroner during the inquest, at its close Henderson and Summons were arrested and on the following day, Thursday 2 September, appeared at Barnsley Borough Court before Councillor Chappell and

Barnsley Market Place c.*1915*. Author's collection

Lieutenant Plumpton. They were charged that they unlawfully and wilfully did neglect certain children under the age of sixteen years; namely Florence Summons aged one year and ten months and John Henderson Summons aged eight months. Both prisoners pleaded not guilty. Florence Summons carried the child Florence Summons in her arms.

Mr E J F Rideal prosecuted on behalf of the NSPCC and said Henderson and Summons had been under observation since September 1914, when they were lodging at the *Silver Pan* in Shambles Street. At that time they had only on child, the one that the prisoner, Summons, now had in her arms. Mr Rideal said that because of the child's dirty and neglected condition Inspector Chappell had to repeatedly caution the mother. Regarding the dead child, it was proved at the inquest that its death was hastened by the parents' neglect. The child did not weigh what it should weigh normally and young as the child was, the mother used to leave him alone in the house and remonstrations by neighbours and warnings by the NSPCC, were to no avail. Mr Rideal said the prisoners could consider themselves lucky that they were not in court on a charge of manslaughter.

Inspector Chappell said he had the defendants under observation for a year and on one particular occasion had insisted that the mother take the child, Florence Summons, to the Beckett

Hospital to have her eyes treated, which she did but only under pressure. The deceased child, John Henderson Summons, was healthy at birth but his condition had deteriorated considerably during his short life. Inspector Chappell said he had remonstrated time after time with the parents but to no avail. He added, that in fact they had gone from bad to worse.

Laura Summons said:

I did my best for the child, but I had no money to do it.

Inspector Chappell said that he visited the defendants' house at 21 Cooper Street and found the baby John Henderson Summons lying across a couple of chairs and quite alone. The mother would be out for hours at a time, and when she told him that Henderson would not give her money, Inspector Chappell said he advised her to summon him for an order, but this she refused to do.

One of the defendants' neighbours, Emily Johnson, said that Henderson and Summons were constantly quarrelling and she had heard Summons say to Henderson:

You can do what you like to the child upstairs [meaning the deceased baby].

Emily Johnson went on to say that there had been no peace in the neighbourhood since the defendants went to live there and that their house was dirty.

Mrs Shirt, a milk dealer, said she advised Laura Summons to take her baby to a doctor as he was getting worse every day.

Medical evidence was provided by Dr Howell, who said the baby's death was undoubtedly due to neglect. Dr Howell told the court that he had conducted a post-mortem examination on John Henderson Summons. He weighed only seven pounds instead of the fourteen pounds he should have weighed normally.

Asked if they had anything to say Henderson and Summons simply blamed each other. The chairman, Councillor Chappell, in addressing the prisoners said in view of the sharp sentences which had been meted out recently the bench had thought they had got to the bottom of this evil, but apparently that was not the case. He told them that their conduct had been disgraceful and sentenced them to three months in prison each, with hard labour.

High Street, Grimethorpe, seen here in the early twentieth-century. Grimethorpe Colliery was situated about a hundred yards further down the street.
Chris Sharp of Old Barnsley.

NIPPER LAMPS DEPUTY, GRIMETHORPE, 1919
... injury to the deputy resulted in him being off work for two days.

A fifteen-year-old lad from Grimethorpe appeared in the Children's Court at Barnsley in February 1919. Described as a 'nipper' (boy miner) by occupation, the lad appeared in connection with a breach of the Coal Mines Act. Mr Falwasser told the court that the lad had struck a deputy at Grimethorpe Colliery on the top of his head with a lamp following the deputy having reported him for some offence. The injury to the deputy resulted in him being off work for two days. The nipper was fined £2 with the stipulation that £1 of the fine was to go to the deputy as compensation for the injuries he sustained.

MURDER AND SUICIDE, CARLTON, 1921
... suggested that when her throat was cut she had put her hand to the wound, and then had attempted to rise and slithered down the wall.

Following their arrival from Canada in 1914, having been resident in Carlton since that time, where they found sanctuary, by January 1921 George Hitchie and his wife, Maria, had settled down well and were highly regarded by the local community. Romanian by birth, they had decided to settle in England after the projected return to their homeland was thwarted by the outbreak of the First World War.

Thirty-eight-year-old George Hitchie worked as a colliery labourer at Monckton Main. He and his thirty-nine-year-old wife, Maria, lived at Back Mason's Row, Carlton, and four pit lads aged from sixteen to eighteen lodged with them. On the night of the murder and suicide at their home in Back Mason's Row the four lads were at work. George Hitchie had worked regularly until about a week before the tragedy occurred but recently he had been ill and depressed. He spent most of Wednesday 25 January sitting in the house holding his head between his hands. Wednesday was his wife's washing day and she was up ironing clothes until late. She had supper at her next door neighbour's house and when she left her neighbour, Mrs Bill, Maria was in a cheerful mood.

On Thursday morning, 26 January, Mrs Bill got up and, as she habitually did, rapped on the wall between her house and that of the Hitchies to inform them that it was getting up time. She got no answer to her repeated knockings. When the four lodgers returned to the Hitchies' house at about 6.15am they found no one up. The lads, together with Mrs Bill and a man named Horner, tried to force the door. This proved difficult so Mr Horner entered through a downstairs window and opened the door from the inside. The party continued upstairs with Mrs Bill leading the way. She was stopped in her tracks as she entered the Hitchies bedroom and beheld the appalling scene there. Maria Hitchie was lying face downwards on the bed. George Hitchie's legs were on the floor, with his body huddled against the bed, his almost severed head on the quilt. There were no signs of a struggle but the bloodstains on the wall near where Maria Hitchie had been accustomed to sleep, suggested that when her throat was cut she had put her hand to the wound, and then had attempted to rise and slithered down the wall. The bloodstained razor which had evidently been used to cut both Maria and her husband's throat was near George Hitchie's foot.

The police were informed and Inspector Lees and Dr Pare of Royston were quickly at the scene. Mrs Bill gave a statement to Inspector Lees:

> *When I wake up I always knock on the wall to wake up Mrs Hitchie, so that she can make the fire and get ready the boys' meal. This morning I got no reply, and after knocking again and getting no reply I said, 'I think there is something devilishly wrong.' The boys returned from work about a quarter past six and could not get in. After they had waited some time I said, 'It is no good; there is something wrong: let's make the door fly.' The boys and a neighbour named Mr B. Horner tried to force the door open, and not being able to they forced a window. Mr Horner went through the window and came and opened the door. I went through after them. Downstairs we found nothing out of place. We went upstairs, Mr Horner behind me, and discovered the tragedy. When I saw them, I said, 'My God he has done her in.' He was leaned half-on and half-off the bed with his throat cut from ear to ear. There was blood everywhere. He had turned the bedclothes up to the wound and both he and his wife were in night attire. The razor was by his foot on the floor. His wife was laid on her stomach with her hands hanging out of bed. It looked as if she had got up and slipped down the wall back on to the bed. Her throat was severed from ear to ear. I have never seen such a sight in my life… I heard no one in the night. She had supper with me last night and was with me until a quarter to eleven. She was with Mrs Jones, another neighbour, until a quarter to twelve. She appeared to be in her usual good health, but her husband had been suffering a long time and had been under a doctor. They had their 'nags' [rows] which most married people have, but lived comfortably together. She was a good woman, and I heard nothing last night up to twelve o'clock. She was one of the cleanest and most honest women who ever broke bread.*

An inquest was held on Saturday 28 January at the *Wharncliffe Arms*, Carlton, before Mr C J Haworth, coroner. Superintendent McDonald was present at the inquiry, as was Mr W Humphries who intimated that the Monckton Branch of the Yorkshire Miners' Association would be responsible for the funeral.

William Daye Powe, pony driver, told the inquest he had been lodging with the Hitchies for about two months. He said he left the house on Wednesday night at 9.30pm to go to work. Mr and Mrs Hitchie were in the house and although he couldn't understand what they were saying because they were speaking in their own language, he got the impression they were quarrelling. He went on to say that the Hitchies generally seemed to get on well together, then added that Mr Hitchie had been unwell for about a week and was very depressed and complained of pains in his head.

Mary Ellen Jones, wife of Harold Jones, miner, who lived next door to the Hitchies, and had known them for several years, said that they appeared to get on well together. She went on to say that for the last week George Hitchie had 'looked queer'. On Wednesday night at about 10pm she had asked him if he was ill and he had replied that he had pains in his inside. At about 11.45pm Maria Hitchie came to her house and stayed for an hour talking but made no reference to her husband's condition. Mrs Jones said she went to bed and at about 4.50am on Thursday morning she was awakened by a bump, which appeared to come from the next house. Mrs Jones said she then heard groans but these soon ceased, so she thought no more about it and went back to sleep.

Benjamin Horner, coke drawer, who lived next door but one to the Hitchies said they had seemed to live fairly comfortably. He described the events of the morning the bodies were discovered and described how he had assisted Mrs Bill and the Hitchie's lodgers to gain entry to the house. Mr Horner added that when he had spoken to George Hitchie on Monday night he appeared to be happy.

Police Constable Smith said he had known the Hitchies for some time and had not noticed anything peculiar about them. They always appeared to be attached to each other. He said he saw the bodies at 7.30am on Thursday morning. There was a pool of blood in the middle of the bed and a stream of blood across the floor to the door from the woman's head. Constable Smith produced the bloodstained razor, which was found lying by the man's foot.

Dr H B Pare said he had attended George Hitchie about six months ago. The doctor went on to say that when Hitchie was ill he was very depressed, although his ailments were only minor ones. Both Hitchie and his wife enjoyed fairly good health. Dr Hitchie saw the two deceased at 8.15am on

Thursday morning and they appeared to have been dead for about four hours. He said the man was lying diagonally across the bed with his head in the centre. He turned him over and found an incised wound across the throat, which had severed the veins on the left side of the neck and the artery on the same side. These wounds could have been self-inflicted with the razor produced. There were no other marks on the body. The woman was lying on the other side of the bed near the walls. There was an incised wound stretching from low down in the neck across the front to behind the opposite ear. The arteries, veins and trachea were severed. There was no other mark of violence on the body except a slight wound on the knuckle of the middle finger of the right hand, which might have been done the day before death. Dr Pare said the wounds to the woman's throat in his opinion could not have been self-inflicted. The cause of death in both cases was haemorrhage from the injuries.

Dr Pare said in the case of the man the wound was practically straight across the throat, but was deeper on the right side. In the case of the woman the incision was diagonally across the neck, commencing low down on the left side and stretching to a point behind the right ear. Dr Pare said he believed when the attack occurred the woman was lying slightly on her left side and the wound was inflicted from behind and slightly above.

In summing up, the coroner told the jury that there was not much evidence to consider but what little evidence there was, was very important. They had before them the case of two people who bore excellent character and had caused no trouble. The week previously the deceased man had been depressed. William Daye Powe had described how he believed the Hitchies might have been quarrelling on Wednesday night. They might have been having a few words or they might have been having a friendly discussion. Dr Pare has told us that in the case of the woman her injuries could not have been self-inflicted but with regard to the man he thought they might very well have been self-inflicted. The coroner said to the jury that it was for them to decide how these injuries had come about. After consulting together the jury decided that the woman was murdered by her husband who afterwards committed suicide whilst of unsound mind and the coroner recorded that verdict.

LARCENY AT PENISTONE, 1921
... forced entry into the hut by means of a screwdriver.

In August 1921 William F Guttridge, one time labourer at the Penistone steelworks of Messrs Cammell Laird and Co, found himself in the dock before magistrates Alderman J F Horne (Chairman) and Mr J White at Barnsley West Riding Police Court. He pleaded guilty to a charge of stealing seventeen bed rugs from his former employers and expressed his sorrow and deep regret for having done so.

Superintendent Blacker said the rugs were stolen from the steelworks and were of a total value of £4. Cammell Laird and Co had been extending their premises and in order to accommodate the workmen employed by the contractor, some huts had been erected and each workman was provided with a bed, some sheets and some blankets. Guttridge had been appointed caretaker and his wife and daughter engaged to clean the huts. During mid-June work ceased and the workforce, including Guttridge, were paid off. At 9.00pm on Saturday 13 August the works detective and night watchmen were inspecting the premises when they heard a noise in one of the huts. When they went inside they saw Guttridge. He had

An early twentieth century view of Penistone. Chris Sharp of Old Barnsley

taken down ten blankets from a shelf and made ready to take them away. He had forced entry into the hut by means of a screwdriver. Police later discovered seven more blankets at Gutteridge's home, which indicated that he must have previously visited the hut and purloined the items. Superintendent Blacker told the court that the prisoner was previously of good character. After deliberating for a while, the chairman delivered the verdict. Mr Horne told Guttridge that his character had saved him from going to gaol. He was fined 40s. and costs.

❧

CLEVER DECEPTION AT WOMBWELL, 1922
Jones admitted in Court that she had written this bogus document herself.

On Friday 8 September 1922, Mrs Lillian Jones, of no fixed address appeared at Barnsley West Riding Court before Mr W Dutson (Chairman) Mr W Lax and Mr G A Griffiths. She pleaded guilty to three charges of obtaining money by false pretences from three married ladies: Ethel Whitehead and Alice Scott, living at the same address, 30 Edward Street, Wombwell; and Mary Corton of 34 Edward Street. Superintendent Blacker told the court that there were other charges against Lillian Jones which would be dealt with at a later date as she had not hesitated to adopt more than one method of obtaining money.

Lillian Jones went to live with Mrs Whitehead in Edward Street in May 1922 with her husband and for the first two weeks she paid 6s. board for her husband and herself. Shortly afterwards the deception began. Jones showed Mrs Whitehead a document purporting to be her mother's will by which she was soon to inherit a sum of money in the region of £1,700. Jones admitted in court that she had written this bogus document herself. As a result of seeing this will Mrs Whitehead advanced Jones £3. Jones also told Mrs Whitehead that a neighbour named Mrs Haslehurst was leaving the district and that she could obtain the house and furniture for her and let her pay for it by easy instalments. This led Mrs Whitehead to give Jones a further 8s. Jones also told the story of the will to Mrs Scott and obtained 5s. from her. Jones followed this up with the story of the house and furniture and managed to obtain a further 7s. from Mrs Scott.

In the third case Jones went to Mrs Corton's house and told

her that her husband had to appear before his union at a public house in Wombwell. She asked Mrs Corton for money to redeem his clothes from the pawnbrokers. Mrs Corton gave her 7s. After obtaining this money on 15 July Jones absconded with her husband and travelled up and down the country until she was eventually tracked down in Nottingham. Everything she had told the three women from whom she had obtained money was found to be untrue. Jones told the court:

I am very sorry for what I have done; I have never been in such a position before.

The three women deceived by Jones gave evidence. Mrs Scott said when she saw the supposed will, as well as a sum in the region of £1,700 the will stated there were also two houses to be divided between Lillian Jones and her two brothers. At this point Jones appeared to be overcome with emotion and said:

I have never been in such a position before. I throw myself on your mercy, and every shilling I will pay. Give me one chance.

The chairman said the bench was anxious to give her a chance but they could not have her impose on other people. She had told some very glaring lies and the Bench must mark their disapproval of this type of case. Lillian Jones was given a three-month prison sentence. On hearing the sentence she was so distraught that she had to be assisted from the dock.

❦

BOOKMAKER FINED FOR STREET BETTING, WORTLEY, 1922
The constable saw the cyclist put the slips of paper into an envelope and seal it.

At 3.30pm on 31 August 1922, a police constable saw a man riding a bicycle through Wortley in the direction of Deepcar. The cyclist approached two men, spoke to them and dismounted. The two men handed the cyclist slips of paper and what appeared to be money. The constable saw the cyclist put the slips of paper into an envelope and seal it. He also put the envelope and the money into his pocket. He then remounted and rode off. He was stopped by the constable and the envelope was found to contain twelve betting slips relating to twenty-two horses running in races at York later that day. He also had £2 1s. 10½d. in his possession. The cyclist was Reginald Beardshall, bookmaker, of Thurgoland. He was summoned to appear before magistrates at Barnsley West Riding Court on Friday 9 September, where he was fined £10 for street betting.

❦

PLATTS COMMON YOUTH ROBBED PARENTS, 1925
If I am let off this time I will not offend again.

On Monday 29 June 1925, the public gallery at Barnsley West Riding Police Court was shocked to hear charges of theft brought against their son by the parents of Platts Common labourer Vincent Lindley. Lindley was charged with stealing £2 6s. from his mother Ethelda Lindley. The bench heard that it was with great difficulty and with much regret that it had become necessary to bring these charges. It was a very painful matter for parents to come forward and testify against their son. Circumstances, however, had overtaken such considerations. On 18 August 1924 Lindley asked his mother for some money but she refused to give him any. She had placed her money in an upstairs chest. Two days later the money was gone.

As recently as 21 June Vincent Lindley had taken a watch and some money from his parents' house. The boy would not listen to reason and in desperation his parents had come to the conclusion that there was no alternative but to bring their son to court to answer for his unacceptable behaviour. However, the bench were told that neither Superintendent Blacker, nor Vincent Lindley's parents wished that he should be severely punished but that if treated with clemency he might be placed on the right track and would not offend again. The stolen watch had since been returned.

Mrs Lindley gave evidence but in the ensuing period between charges being brought and the court hearing she had

clearly changed her mind and did not appear to have any desire to see her son answer for his misdemeanours. She said that her son had been away from home and that she did not know where he was working. There was a distinct degree of animosity in the courtroom between the parents and their son, which as evidence unfolded appeared to be somewhat cooled.

Superintendent Blacker said:

I think he has more than taken the notion that his parents have not treated him quite right. I find there is nothing in it at all.

Vincent Lindley told the bench:

If I am let off this time I will not offend again.

The bench having considered the evidence and having taken into account the apparent shift in the opinions of his parents, nevertheless made a decision based on the evidence presented and the original charge. The chairman, Alderman S Jones commented that it was a most wicked and cruel thing to steal from one's parents and that Vincent Lindley would be bound over for twelve months in the sum of £10.

∽∾∾

COAL STEALING AT CARLTON, 1930
...Key and Pennington pleaded poverty and large families.

On Friday 19 December 1930, Thomas Key, a miner from Cudworth and William Pennington, a labourer from Barnsley appeared at Barnsley West Riding Police Court charged with stealing coal. Police Constable Cowburn gave evidence that he had seen Key and Pennington each with a sack of coal, in the wagon run at the Wharncliffe Woodmoor Colliery, Carlton, a place where notices warning people against trespassing on the sidings were clearly displayed. Both men had bicycles. When approached by Constable Cowburn one of the men remarked:

We are not taking it from the wagons.

Both Key and Pennington pleaded poverty and large families. After due consideration the bench decided on leniency. The men were ordered to pay costs on promising not to offend again.

ROBBERY AND VIOLENT ATTACK ON
POLE AT STAINBOROUGH, 1947
... Gill tendered a bloodstained £5 note to pay for drinks in a Wakefield public house...

On the evening of Saturday 27 September 1947 Julian Wiazewicz, a Pole living at Stainborough camp attended a dance at Thurgoland school. After the dance was over he made his way home. In his wallet was a £5 note and two £1 notes. As he returned to the camp he met three young men. One of the men named Johnson, carried on walking but the other two accosted Mr Wiazewicz and attacked and robbed him. William Gill, aged twenty-one, a builder's labourer from Cliffe Lane, Monk Bretton and Alfred Foster, a nineteen-year-old glassworker from Priory Road, Lundwood battered the Pole about the head with stones and it was to be another eighteen hours before Mr Wiazewicz was found unconscious in a ditch a mile away from the scene of the attack. He was covered in blood and had sustained a fractured skull.

On Sunday 28 September, Gill tendered a bloodstained £5 note to pay for drinks in a Wakefield public house, a large sum of money for such a young man to have in his possession in those days. The bloodstains did not escape the scrutiny of the landlord, who alerted police. This led to Gill and Foster being apprehended and sufficient evidence linked them to the attack on Mr Wiazewicz. On Friday 20 November, Gill and Foster were tried at Leeds Assizes before Mr Justice Morris. They both pleaded guilty to robbery with violence.

Prosecuting, Mr G W Wrangham said:

> *It was a miracle the victim survived the fractured skull after lying throughout the night without attention.*

Both Mr H R H Shepherd defending Gill and D O Swift, defending Foster, said both men had had too much to drink. In passing sentence of three years penal servitude Mr Justice Morris told Gill and Foster that they were very fortunate not to be standing in the dock charged with murder. The judge went on to say:

> *It was a dreadful thing that an innocent man whom you robbed should have been left lying on the ground over eighteen hours and it is shocking that the crime should have been committed by such young men.*

JUMP WOMAN A NUISANCE TO POLICE, 1955
...ten previous convictions for being drunk and incapable or disorderly.

On Thursday 28 July 1955, a fifty-seven-year-old Jump woman stood in the dock at Barnsley Magistrates' Court, before Chairman Alderman A E McVie and magistrates, charged with being drunk and incapable in Sheffield Road, Barnsley. Mrs Alice Ruse, a housewife of 1 Jump Valley, Jump, pleaded guilty. Superintendent R S Harrison, prosecuting said that Alice Ruse had ten previous convictions for being drunk and incapable or disorderly. The superintendent added:

It seems to be a habit.

Police Constable J Edgar told magistrates that he saw Ruse staggering about in Sheffield Road and fall to the ground. She was arrested and had to be assisted both into and out of the police car. Ruse told the court that she came from Hoyland. Her home was in actual fact one of a pair of cottages in Jump Valley, which lies between the township of Hoyland and the village of Jump, in the township of Wombwell. After fining Alice Ruse £1, Alderman McVie told her:

Stay in Hoyland or somewhere else...Stay away from Barnsley...you are becoming a persistent drunk and a nuisance to the police.

∽∾∽

FORTY-FIVE THEFTS COMMITTED BY THREE BARNSLEY SCHOOLGIRLS, 1962
Had you been ashamed of yourselves the first time you would not have repeated it.

Mr A R Keeping, presiding at Barnsley Borough Juvenile Court on Tuesday 3 April 1962 expressed the view that it was difficult to believe that three schoolgirls, all from good homes, could commit a total of forty-five stealing offences between them. In addressing the three girls Mr Keeping said:

You have no shame about it. Had you been ashamed of yourselves the first time you would not have repeated it.

Two of the girls aged twelve admitted stealing goods worth £1 4s. 11d. from two Barnsley stores and jointly with a third girl aged thirteen admitted stealing books worth £1 0s. 8d. One of the twelve-year-olds asked for thirteen similar offences to be taken into consideration, the other eighteen offences and the elder girl seven offences

Chief Inspector L Malkin said that a shop assistant at one particular Barnsley store had seen one of the girls take two purses from a counter, put them in a carrier bag and walk out without paying. Chief Inspector Malkin said the carrier bag and a case which the other girl was carrying contained articles stolen from the two stores. One of the girls told the Chief Inspector:

It was a girl at school who showed us how to steal.

The two twelve-year-olds were fined £6 each and the thirteen-year-old £2.

⚜

BARNSLEY LABOURER'S LIFE OF CRIME, 1962
I began stealing small things and then larger things. I had no intention of stealing but I could not help it.

In April 1962, twenty-six-year-old labourer James Parr of St John's Terrace, Barnsley, stood in the dock at Barnsley Borough Magistrates' Court and pleaded guilty to stealing 170 cigarettes and £2 15s. cash from a cigarette machine outside Agnes Road Post Office, Barnsley, and also to stealing a suede coat valued at £12 from a parked car. He asked for five other offences of stealing to be taken into consideration.

Superintendent R S Harrison said that after Parr was visited at home by police about the theft from the cigarette machine, they found the suede coat in his bedroom. It had been stolen from a car parked overnight in Cope Street, Barnsley. Superintendent Harrison said of Parr:

He has been in trouble far too often. He has nine convictions for stealing and one for burglary, dating from 1950.

Parr told the court that as a boy of eight he had sustained head injuries after he fell 20ft from a lamp standard he had climbed. He said after this accident he had suffered from strange headaches, blackouts and a nervous disorder, then added:

*At the age of thirteen or fourteen I became ill with St Vitus'
Dance. I was ill in bed for two weeks and then my life of crime
began. I began stealing small things and then larger things. I
had no intention of stealing but I could not help it.*

After receiving hospital treatment his tendency to steal stopped.
However, when financial pressures began to get the better of
him the desire to steal returned. Parr told the court:

*I have told no one of this matter, but the time has now come
when you should know, otherwise my life will be spent in
prison. I promise from this day forth I will not appear before
you again.*

Parr said that when he had last come out of prison he had found
it difficult to secure employment. He qualified this by saying:

*As soon as they knew I had just come out of prison they said
"No." I was down and out and I went back to crime again.*

In sentencing Parr to twelve months imprisonment Mrs E
Allum, presiding, told him:

*With a record like yours it is quite apparent that you have no
respect either for the law or for other people's property.*

⤳⤳⤳

FOUND GUILTY OF BEGGING, BARNSLEY, 1962
Please help a disabled soldier – can you spare a copper?

Fifty-nine-year-old Thomas Hill of 1 Cromwell Terrace,
Barnsley, was found guilty of begging and fined £3 at Barnsley
Borough Court in May 1962. Unemployed Hill told the court
that he had had seven operations for the removal of cancerous
tumours and had served during World War Two.

Police Constable Jones told the court that he and another
officer were standing near the entrance to the Eldon Arcade
when they saw Hill with some cards in his hand. They subsequently saw Hill attempt to push one of the cards into the hands
of two young girls, but they walked away. Constable Jones said
that Hill then approached a young man with a card, and as he
did so he was heard to say:

Please help a disabled soldier – can you spare a copper?

Hill denied trying to give the cards to the girls and to the young man. He said he wasn't carrying cards but had a newspaper in his hand.

∽∾∾

CANNABIS ADDICT MURDERS UNCLE, GRIMETHORPE, 1995
...high on cannabis and highly intoxicated, jigged around like a footballer celebrating a goal.

On Tuesday 7 November 1995, twenty-one-year-old Adrian Stewart of Margate Street, Grimethorpe, was given a life sentence at Sheffield Crown Court, for the murder of his thirty-three-year-old uncle Patrick 'Paddy' Kennedy, also of Margate Street. In sentencing Stewart the judge told him he had behaved aggressively due to drink and drugs, but that was no excuse for what he had done.

At the commencement of his trial Stewart pleaded not guilty, claiming he had acted in self-defence. Counsel for the prosecution, Mr Guy Whitburn QC, told the jury that late on the night of 1 June 1994 Patrick Kennedy was stabbed with an eight-inch bladed knife by his nephew. Earlier that evening Adrian Stewart was given £2 by his sister, with which to buy drinks. He attacked her when she refused to give him more money. A while later Stewart was thrown out of Grimethorpe Ex-Servicemen's Club. As he was being ejected from the club he uttered threats against his uncle. It emerged that Stewart had asked a group of teenagers for some tights or stockings. He brandished a knife and said he intended to commit a post office robbery adding that he intended to kill the postmaster unless he handed over £2,000 to him.

Adrian Stewart was by now intoxicated and high on cannabis, Mr Whitburn told the jury that:

He was in an aggressive mood and displaying irrational and bizarre behaviour.

Stewart went to his uncle's home, carrying a piece of wood. He stood outside shouting threats and began running up and down the street. Patrick Kennedy came out of his home armed with a cricket bat. He refused Stewart's request to supply him with tights, then knocked the piece of wood from his nephew's hand and chased him down the street. As Mr Kennedy made his way back home, Stewart came up from behind and as his uncle turned to face him he stabbed him in the chest. The knife punctured his lungs and penetrated his heart. Mr Kennedy died at the scene. While Patrick Kennedy's lifeless body lay on the ground in Margate Street Mr Whitburn said:

> *... his nephew, who was high on cannabis and highly intoxicated, jigged around like a footballer celebrating a goal.*

Stewart later told police that he had only intended to hurt his uncle, but had not intended to kill him.

With overwhelming evidence against him Stewart, who was not called to give evidence on his own behalf, was convicted by an 11-1 majority verdict. Before the judge passed sentence the court was told how Stewart had previous convictions for violence, stealing and possessing amphetamines and that he had attempted suicide in his prison cell on 1 June, the anniversary of his uncle's death. It was only through the vigilance of a prison warder that he was saved after he was quickly cut down and revived.

The judge, Mr Justice Gage, told Stewart:

> *You went out with a knife in your possession. It is obvious you had too much to drink and took drugs but that is no excuse... You behaved in an aggressive manner when Mr Kennedy came to you with a cricket bat because of your behaviour... In the course of that confrontation you murdered him and it is a dreadful crime... You may have shown genuine remorse for what you did but there is only one sentence I can pass and that is life imprisonment.*

After the trial was over Detective Sergeant Ray Turnbull said:

> *If he had not gone into his mum's home and got the knife he would not have been in the dock and found himself convicted of murder... He walked the streets for hours with it in his possession, consumed a lot of alcohol and smoked cannabis... His mum, Patricia Lakin has lost a brother, her son is locked up for life. It must be difficult to know how she must feel today... The eight-inch blade went into his uncle's chest up to the hilt.*

CHAPTER 2

Animal Matters
1860–2007

CAUGHT RUNNING RABBITS, 1860
...threatened to knock Race's brains out if he did
not let it go.

On Wednesday 25 April 1860, William Dickenson and William Haigh, stood in the dock at Barnsley Court House, charged with trespassing on land belonging to Lord Wharncliffe, in search of game. Mr Tyas prosecuted and Mr Harper defended. William Race, one of Lord Wharncliffe's gamekeepers gave evidence that on Sunday 22 April he came across Dickenson and Haigh in West Wood, situated close to his Lordship's home, Wortley Hall, midway between Howbrook and Tankersley. They had a dog with them which was running rabbits. Race said that when the two men noticed him approaching, they fled. However, following Race being successful in capturing the dog, Haigh returned and threatened to 'knock Race's brains out' if he did not let it go. Help was close at hand and Dickenson and Haigh were quickly apprehended. The two men were each fined twenty shillings and costs, which in all amounted to £3 3s., or had the option to spend one month in the House of Correction.

❧

GAME TRESPASS, 1865
...digging with a stake at a rabbit hole.

Another poaching case, which also involved Lord Wharncliffe's land in West Wood, took place in 1865. On Wednesday 29 March, Abraham Longbottom stood in the dock at Barnsley Court House, charged with game trespass. Thomas Magies, an underkeeper, gave evidence that at about 11am on Sunday 19 March, he heard a dog running in West Wood and saw Longbottom digging with a stake at a rabbit hole. Magies said he watched Longbottom for about ten minutes, as he stooped down and put his wrench into the hole, then Longbottom noticed him and ran away. However, he was apprehended and the dog identified as his. He was fined ten shillings and costs, with the option of a month in prison.

❧

OUTRAGED, OF STOCKTON-ON-TEES, 1876
It must be a painful consideration to every feeling mind, that this savage and demoralising practice should have been suffered so long to remain a stain upon the character of our time...

A letter to the editor of the *Barnsley Chronicle* from J Taylor of 4 Cobden Street, Stockton-on-Tees, published on 26 July 1876 gives an interesting insight into life for some in Barnsley and district during the reign of William IV and the early years of Victoria's reign. Mr Taylor states:

Sir, - In your issue of Feb. 5th, I find under the head 'Annals of Barnsley and its Environs,' a record to the following effect: 'On Barnsley Feast Monday (August 22nd, 1831), the last bull baiting was held at Barnsley, on which occasion the bull broke loose.' There must be some mistake here, as I have witnessed in the environs of Barnsley, bull baiting scenes seven or eight years later on. I was born in the city of York, in the year 1828. I was six years of age when I was brought to Barnsley: this of course was in the year 1834. I must have been at least ten years of age when I saw the last bull baiting scene: on that occasion the bull broke loose. This took place on Worsboro' Common, at the top of the lane issuing out of Johnny Wanderer's lane. I have, amongst the few records of olden times, a hand-bill, headed, 'Bull-baiting,' bearing the printer's name, G Harrison, binder &c., Market-hill, Barnsley; which was distributed broadcast. I believe by the members of the Society of Friends. I will give the first and last paragraphs of the bill: 'It must be a painful consideration to every feeling mind, that this savage and demoralising practice should have been suffered so long to remain a stain upon the character of our time; and to be annually renewed with all its attendant enormities without even an effort being made to stem the tide of wanton barbarity.' After dwelling upon the enormity of the evil, it concluded thus: 'Under these impressions, I would entreat my fellow townsmen to dismiss forever from the catalogue of their amusements, a practice which, though, perhaps, not amenable to any human tribunal, can hardly fail to be viewed with displeasure by Him whose Almighty power alike created both man and beast.' Believing that the annals generally are correct, I was more surprised to find this circumstance recorded for 1831, because many others in Barnsley will remember this brutal amusement, seeing that it has occurred since that year. It strikes me that the record to which I refer, may be explained as being the last case as an annual custom. I often think of Barnsley as it was about 35 years ago, and witnessed not only bull baiting but badger baiting, hedgehog and cat worrying, and many other cruel sports conducted in the public streets, which would not now be tolerated. Barnsley has improved wonderfully in matters of this kind, but it still has a foul stain upon its character, so long as it tolerates in that most cruel of all sports – rabbit coursing. Is it not horrible to find men so cruel and debased as to glut their savage souls by witnessing two or three dogs tear a lovely rabbit asunder? Men who are so cruel are unsafe as members of a civilized community.

CARTER AND DRIVER FOUND GUILTY
OF ILL-TREATING HORSES, 1892
The horses were in a poor state and were unable to pull
the cartload of bricks to which they were attached.

On Wednesday 27 January 1892, John Robert Worrall, carter and David Gash, driver, were charged with ill-treating a horse at Barnsley Police Court. The Mayor (Alderman Blackburn) presided. The court was told that Worrall was charged with having caused a horse to be cruelly ill-treated by working it in an unfit state. Gash was charged with having worked the horse. Police Constable Underwood said that on Saturday 23 January he saw Gash in Brinkman Street (Sheffield Road), Barnsley, in charge of two horses. The horses were in a poor state and were unable to pull the cartload of bricks to which they were attached. The constable examined the horses and found a sore on the shoulder of one of them from which puss and matter was issuing. It was apparent that the animal was suffering great pain. The constable's evidence was corroborated by Constable Fowlie. The defendants admitted the offence. Worrall, the horse's owner said that the animal always had a poor appearance and that last Monday he had had it destroyed. The Mayor told Worrall that the bench were doubtful whether or not to send him to prison but in the end decided to fine him 40*s.* and costs, or one month; Gash was fined 5*s.* and costs, or fourteen days.

༔

THEFT OF COCKEREL RESULTS IN
IMPRISONMENT, GAWBER, 1907
...he traced some footprints to within a short distance of
George Fox's house.

In January 1907, George William Fox, an engine tenter, from Gawber found himself in the dock at Barnsley Borough Court charged with stealing a Plymouth Rock cockerel and a black Minorca hen. Both birds were the property of Harry Moss, a miner, who also lived at Gawber. On the night of Monday 14 January Mr Moss had securely locked the hen house but the next morning he found that it had been broken into. The black hen was found dead on the floor of the hen house, its neck having been wrung. The cockerel was missing. Police Constable King was informed and on visiting the scene he traced some footprints to within a short distance of George Fox's house. At first Fox

denied any knowledge of the fowls but subsequently admitted that he had been drinking brandy and afterwards did not know what he was doing. He took the constable to a field belonging to Mr Brady, where he had thrown the dead cockerel. Fox told the bench that he regretted having broken into the hen house and pleaded for leniency. He was sentenced to one month in prison.

✺

MINER'S CRUELTY TO A PONY, BIRDWELL, 1907
... a chestnut pony attached to a greengrocer's cart
being driven whilst it was clearly in a state of distress.

Police Constable Morphet was on duty in Birdwell on the afternoon of 23 February 1907 when he saw a chestnut pony attached to a greengrocer's cart being driven whilst it was clearly in a state of distress. The pony was very lame on the off foreleg and, as later discovered, suffered from ringbone. The driver, Matthew Boreham, a former miner from Hoyland was arrested for having cruelly ill-treated the animal by working it when it was in an unfit state. After further investigations both Matthew

An Edwardian view of Birdwell, where Matthew Boreham was arrested for ill-treating his pony. Chris Sharp of Old Barnsley

Boreham and his father Seth Boreham, a miner, were summoned to appear before magistrates at Barnsley Borough Court on Friday 22 March. Inspector Street of the RSPCA said such was its condition that the pony was unable to do even light work. Police Constable Morphet and Thomas Henry Greenwood gave evidence as to seeing the animal worked. It was pointed out that the pony belonged to the son and not the father and it was revealed that Seth Boreham had bought the pony for his son to help him in his new business venture on account of him being no longer able to work at the mine due to his failing eyesight. Magistrates deemed both father and son to be culpable for the sorry state of the pony and fined each of them 10*s*. and costs.

∽∾∾

FOWL AND THEFT, ARDSLEY, 1919
… twenty-seven fowls had been put in the hen house and not long afterwards three were missing.

Thomas Jordan, a miner from Grimethorpe, at the time off work on compensation, appeared before magistrates at Barnsley West Riding Court in February 1919 and admitted stealing three fowls valued at 45*s*. The fowls were the property of

Frederick M Thirkell of Ardsley. The evidence presented in court showed that twenty-seven fowls had been put in the hen house and not long afterwards three were missing. Jordan had been assisting in delivering the fowls. Mrs Austin, living off Wood Street, Barnsley, said that Jordan had called at her house and offered two pullets for sale. He told her he had killed them because he had had a row with his landlady. She paid him 11s. for the fowls. The curator of the Irish National Club in Barnsley told the court that he had been offered a chicken, when the prisoner had called into the club. Jordan had told him that he was moving from Grimethorpe to Barnsley and he had no room at his new house for fowls so he was killing them. Jordan received 6s. for that bird. Jordan pleaded that he was drunk at the time he took the fowls. The bench fined him 40s.

⁓⌒⁓

ILL-TREATMENT OF A PONY, RYHILL, 1929
...it was very lame and had no shoe on the off hind foot, which was very sore and swollen.

On 20 December 1929, Police Constable Jenkinson was on duty in Ryhill, when he saw a man in charge of a flat cart, heavily laden with coal and drawn by an aged pony. The constable observed that the pony was severely distressed and, having asked the driver to stop, he examined the animal. He found that it was very lame and had no shoe on the off hind foot, which was very sore and swollen. It was clear that the pony was unfit for work and Constable Jenkinson told the driver to unharness it. The driver was Arthur Selby, a pit hand and a resident of Ryhill. He was summoned to appear at Barnsley West Riding Magistrates' Court on Friday 24 January 1930 charged with cruelty to a pony. After hearing the evidence the chairman of the bench asked:

What has become of the pony now?

Arthur Selby replied:

I don't know. I had only borrowed it to fetch some coal for an old lady that is on the parish.

The chairman then asked:

Did you know that it had a shoe missing?

Arthur Selby replied:

No. Not until just before the constable stopped me.

The bench having deliberated for a while, the chairman addressed Selby:

This is a bad case; we don't believe your story. It is a cruel thing to drive a dumb animal whilst in an unfit condition, and you will be fined 40s. and costs.

OUTRAGEOUS CRUELTY.

Dog Dragged Behind Lorry.

DOG CRUELLY DRAGGED BEHIND LORRY, HOYLAND COMMON, 1930
The dog was being dragged along and on two occasions Mr Hough said he saw it pulled completely off its feet.

At 7.15pm on 26 May 1930, engineer Albert Edward Rose of Parkgate, Sheffield was driving his car through Hoyland Common in the direction of Barnsley when he saw a lorry approaching from the opposite direction. As he drew nearer the lorry he noticed a dog was running behind it, attached by a cord and it was apparent the animal was in a very distressed condition as the lorry was travelling at a faster speed than the dog could reasonably be expected to run. A little further up the road Mr Rose reported what he had seen at Birdwell Police Station. Police Constable Gascoigne went to investigate and found the lorry and driver. George T Kaye was a haulage contractor from Hoyland Common. When Constable Gascoigne interviewed Kaye he remarked:

Yes. I had my dog tied behind my lorry. He is frightened of motors.

Constable Gascoigne examined the dog and noticed that it was distressed. There was a red patch on its leg and it was frothing at the mouth. When the constable told Kaye he would be reported, Kaye replied:

I know that it is not right to drag a dog along a road like that.

George Kaye was summoned to appear at Barnsley West Riding Police Court on Monday 2 June 1930. Mr Rose gave evidence for the prosecution as did Robert Hough, a miner, of Warren Hill, who told the court he had seen the lorry travelling along at a fast speed. The dog was being dragged along and on two occasions Mr Hough said he saw it pulled completely off its feet.

Mr K M Walker defending Kaye explained that Kaye had bought the dog from a butcher who lived about 200 yards away. He needed the animal as a watchdog on his allotments, but the dog could not settle and kept returning to the home of its former master. On the day in question Kaye had called for the dog as it had again escaped and returned to the butcher. He said he placed it inside the lorry but did not know how it came to be running on the road, but he asked the bench to bear in mind that the distance covered was only 200 yards. In announcing the bench's decision, the chairman, Mr S Jones, expressed their

Sheffield Road, Hoyland Common. On 26 May 1930 Albert Rose was driving towards the camera in the direction of Birdwell, when he saw a dog being dragged in the opposite direction, attached by a cord to a lorry. Chris Sharp of Old Barnsley

appreciation of the public-spirited action of Mr Rose. He then addressed Kaye and told him:

> *The bench take a very serious view of this case. It was an outrageous thing to do, and we consider that it was done with guilty knowledge. You will have to pay a fine of 40s. and costs.*

∽∾∽

POACHERS CAUGHT NEAR HOWSE'S CORNER, ELSECAR, 1930
Don't make any bother. Tek' one and say nowt.

At 5.40pm on Friday 5 December 1930, Police Constable Brown was pounding his beat at Elsecar. As he walked down Fitzwilliam Street towards Howse's Corner at the junction of Wentworth Road he noticed two men coming towards him from the direction of the Low Wood, situated about 400 yards away. He observed that the bottoms of their trousers were wet and their boots were covered with clay. Arthur Hague of Hoyland and William Ruse of Barnsley, both miners, were searched and Hague was found to have three newly killed pheasants in his possession. Ruse said to Constable Brown:

> *Don't make any bother. Tek' one and say nowt.*

On being charged with a breach of the Poaching Prevention Act

Hague replied:

It's a bit of bad luck we're having.

During the course of conversation that followed Constable Brown told the men he had expected to find pheasants in their possession. The two men appeared at Barnsley West Riding Police Court on Friday Dedcember 19 before Mr G Norman (chairman), Mr W Lax, Mr N Mell and Mr G Shone. Hague told the court that he and Ruse had bought the pheasants off a man with a cart for 6s., which was all the money they had on them at the time. Mr Norman observed that Hague had been up before Barnsley magistrates forty-four times, chiefly for being drunk and disorderly, using obscene language and gaming offences, but he had never been up for poaching before. Ruse, however, had been up thirty-seven times, including ten times for poaching. The magistrates deliberated for a few minutes before fining Hague 40s. and costs. Ruse was sent to prison for one month without the option of a fine.

Looking up Fitzwilliam Street from Howse's Corner, Elsecar, where Police Constable Brown apprehended Arthur Hague and William Ruse, and charged them with a breach of the Poaching Prevention Act, on Friday 5 December 1930.
Chris Sharp of Old Barnsley

STARVING DOG ATE RUBBER TUBING
AND RAGS, PENISTONE, 1948
...the animal had suffered greatly due to Goddard's severe neglect.

On Sunday 26 September 1948, a woman was passing the back yard of Ernest Goddard's house in Sheffield Road, Penistone, when she noticed a black and white sheep dog which was clearly unwell. The following day the dog was still lying there. When the woman went past again on the 30th the dog was still there. It was lying in the middle of the yard on the bars of a sink. Another woman came and saw the dog and reported the matter to the police.

Investigations revealed that a Mrs D Burns had owned a black and white sheep dog named Bruce. It had strayed on several occasions and had once been brought back to her by a member of Goddard's household. In July the dog had strayed again and she had gone to Goddard's house to see if it was there. She was told it was not, but a week later she saw a member of Goddard's household with the dog. After information was given to police about the condition of the dog they visited him. Ernest Goddard said:

I have had the dog about six weeks. It had a dish of bread and milk this morning. It ate it ravenously.

Police took the dog away and such was its poor state of health that it was destroyed later in the day. A post-mortem examination was carried out. In the stomach were found pieces of rag, rubber tubing and a matchstick.

Ernest Goddard appeared before Barnsley magistrates on Wednesday 8 December, charged with causing unnecessary suffering to a dog and with not having a licence. The prosecution said that due to Goddard's neglect the dog was driven to eat rubber tubing, rags and matchsticks and that the animal had suffered greatly due to Goddard's severe neglect. Goddard did not comment about the neglect but simply told the court he was not in a position to have the dog destroyed as it was not his property. Found guilty as charged, Goddard was fined £3 and costs.

APPALLING CRUELTY TO RACE HORSES AT DODWORTH HALL, 1951

Whatever else might emerge in the case and whatever might be the cause of the condition of the animals, one thing stands out very prominently, and that is that the eight horses concerned were found in a deplorably bad condition.

Richard Whittington Asquith, aged twenty-seven, described as an agent, of Dodworth Hall, Dodworth and Ethel Whittington Asquith, aged seventy, a lady of independent means, also of Dodworth Hall were summoned to appear at Barnsley West Riding Court in May 1951 charged with causing unnecessary suffering to horses. Both pleaded not guilty to the charges.

The horses in question were several bloodstock racing horses which were found in a poor condition by an RSPCA inspector. Mr W Winter, prosecuting for the RSPCA told the court:

Whatever else might emerge in the case and whatever might be the cause of the condition of the animals, one thing stands out

Dodworth Hall, the home of Mrs Ethel Whittington Asquith.
Chris Sharp of Old Barnsley

very prominently, and that is that the eight horses concerned
were found in a deplorably bad condition.

The court heard that on 16 January Inspector W E Tillett of the
Barnsley RSPCA, went to the stables at Dodworth Hall to make
an inspection of the eight horses there. During the inspection he
came across a brown foal colt in an open-fronted building. The
animal was down on the floor and unable to get up to its feet.
All the horse was able to do was to pull itself along the floor with
its fore-feet. The young horse appeared to have been eating its
own bedding of wheat straw and its body was severely wasted.
In the next stable was another horse which the inspector could
find no fault with but next door to that was a brown gelding in
a very poor condition and it had nothing in the way of bedding.
In a nearby garage, which had at one time been used for keeping
pigs, Inspector Tillett found a brown mare whose body was in a
poor condition. Next the inspector came across a bay mare,
with nothing provided on the floor for bedding, and the place
itself was of insufficient size to hold such an animal.

In the next stable, another converted garage, which had
previously been used as a coal house, the floor still being
covered with coal dust, was a grey mare. There was also a colt
which was in poor condition and lying down in a three-standing
stable was a brown mare. This horse was groaning and kicking.
On further examination this mare was found to be sweating
profusely and to have a distended stomach; and appeared to be
suffering from colic. The inspector fetched some straw from
another stable and covered the animal to keep it warm. There
was little straw anywhere to be found and stable management
did not appear to exist. A search was made for food but only
bales of wheat straw, a thing horses would not normally eat, was
found.

Inspector Tillett visited the stables again with a veterinary
surgeon. The next day they returned and the brown foal and brown
mare were slaughtered. When Richard Whittington Asquith was
approached about the condition of the horses, he said:

It is not my responsibility.

When Ethel Whittington Asquith was seen by Inspector Tillett,
she told him:

I love these horses. I have bred them. They have not been neglected.

When the inspector asked her if Richard Whittington Asquith was her agent, she replied:

He looks after them but he has only been back a week.

On 23 January, the six remaining horses were removed to racing stables at Tyram Hall at Hatfield, Doncaster, where the owners were so perturbed about their condition that they too called in the RSPCA. Four of the horses were emaciated and there was no doubt that this was due to malnutrition. In court, Mr Winter prosecuting, said that experts had informed him that the proper minimum amount of food for a horse is approximately five pounds of corn and ten pounds of hay per day. These horses had been receiving about one-fifth of that amount over a long period.

Mrs Mary Parks of Dodworth Hall Yard, a tenant of the Asquiths told the court that she and her thirteen-year-old son had looked after the horses at one time. During one six weeks period there had been no hay available. There had been only chop and wheat straw with which to feed the horses.

Mr Winter said:

One of the troubles here was that there has been a certain amount of niggardliness on the part of Mrs Asquith in providing the money to buy food and that, I think, you will find to be the basic cause of this trouble.

Mrs Parks went on to say that at one time Mrs Asquith had asked her son to clean out the horses for 2s. 6d. a week. She added that she had not been the person who reported the matter to the RSPCA and she said she particularly wished to emphasise this point as Mrs Asquith had since given her notice to quit.

Another witness, Violet Lamphar, told the court that she had at times ordered the food for Mrs Asquith's horses and had had some trouble on occasions in getting the money from her,

If she had other things on her mind.

Veterinary Surgeon Mr C J Waters, of Thorne Road, Doncaster, told the Court that he saw the six horses after they had been removed from Dodworth Hall to Tyram Hall. With two exceptions, he said, the horses looked like ghosts.

Richard Whittington Asquith told the court:

I have seen the horses at the Hall but I'm not particularly interested in horses…I have taken the responsibility for this matter hoping to keep Mrs Asquith out of court. I did not go back to Dodworth Hall until after Christmas and the horses must have deteriorated.

Mrs Asquith told the court that there had been a bad winter and that she had had difficulty getting through it. Previously she had spent a lot of money on food for the horses but this winter she might have been a bit more careful. She had been over burdened with her recent divorce and had been trying to get her farms at Scarborough into shape. Having entered horses she had not let them go to the racecourse because it was a waste of time and a waste of money. Mrs Asquith concluded by saying the last thought in her head was that the horses should suffer.

Richard Whittington Asquith was found guilty and fined £25 and ordered to pay £30 4s. costs. Ethel Whittington Asquith was also fined £25 and ordered to pay similar costs for permitting the first offence.

～∂◌∽

KICKED PUPPY TO DEATH, 1962
… kicked it across the room and then down the back steps.

In February 1962 a twenty-eight-year-old unemployed man appeared before magistrates at Barnsley West Riding Court for cruelly ill-treating a puppy by kicking it to death. Gerald Orwin of 4 Holgate Mount, Ward Green, pleaded guilty to the charge.

Chief Inspector J Bradshaw said police officers going to Orwin's home found the dog's carcase about 10ft from the back door. Orwin told them:

I didn't mean to do it – I can't help getting into a bad temper.

Veterinary Surgeon Mr J Marshall said the puppy had bruises above the eyes, its skull was cracked and some ribs were bruised.

In a statement Orwin said he was chastising one of his three children when the dog got under his feet. He kicked it across the room and then down the back steps. He said he suffered from epilepsy and had fits. He got depressed and downhearted and couldn't help getting into a bad temper.

Orwin told the magistrates:

I didn't intend doing that to the dog. I am sorry.

He was fined £10 and ordered to pay £2 2s. costs. He was also banned from keeping a dog for ten years. Mr T Burrows (chairman) told Orwin: 'It was a callous thing to do – you really should have gone to prison.'

༄༅

PET CHIHUAHUA MAULED TO DEATH, JUMP VALLEY, 2007

On the morning of Saturday 23 June 2007, eighty-year-old Laurence Ball of Eaden Crescent, Hoyland, was walking his sixteen-year-old Chihuahua, Kelly, in Jump Valley. A man was also walking five greyhounds nearby. An eyewitness, Paul Murphy of Green Street, Hoyland, told the *Barnsley Chronicle*, while out walking his dog he saw a man struggling to control five greyhounds:

The man had three in one hand and two in the other. They all had muzzles on but one managed to get his off and ran towards the elderly man…It must have thought the dog was a rabbit because it picked it [up] and started dragging it along…It wasn't pretty at all. The poor little dog had no chance.

Mr Murphy hurried over to help but the greyhound kept running off with the Chihuahua in its mouth as he approached it. Then a second greyhound escaped from the dog walker and joined in. By the time both dogs let go of the little dog it was dead. Mr Murphy said he believed the dog walker was unaware of the tragic outcome caused by his greyhounds escaping, he added:

He had run after them and was at the other side of the field so I don't think he knew. But I think if he can't control them he shouldn't be taking them out.

Mr Ball's fifty-four-year-old stepdaughter, Janet Hinchcliffe, of Manor Way, Hoyland, who until its death two years ago owned a Chihuahua, Sparky, from the same litter as Kelly, when interviewed by the *Barnsley Chronicle* said:

> *We know he was old but he didn't deserve to go like that so if anyone has any information then please come forward.*

It later emerged that the man was walking the greyhounds for their female owner, who lived near Greenfield School. If nothing else this unpleasant incident serves a purpose in that it clearly illustrates the foolhardiness of one person being in charge of so many dogs at one time, particularly such a large breed as greyhounds.

CHAPTER 3

Suicides,
1876–1989

LYNCH LAW AT BARNSLEY, 1876
*...led astray by a young man living only yards
away from her own home.*

On 25 October 1876 Mrs Eliza Ann Downing of Somerset Street drowned herself in the canal. She left a sheet of paper on the canal bank on which she had written that she had been led astray by a young man living only yards away from her own home. The young man's identity being known to neighbours, he had since been subjected to much taunting and derision, resulting in him deciding to leave Somerset Street and move to Dodworth. The young man concerned was Tom Dowing, a debt collector. As he prepared to leave Somerset Street late on 28 October a large crowd had gathered opposite his house. At

Lynch Law in Barnsley. Tom Dowing being given a ducking at Town End, Barnsley on 28 October 1876. The Illustrated Police News

about midnight, the crowd, composed chiefly of women burnt and effigy of Dowing. As he prepared to leave the house with his box he was knocked down and kicked several times. He was then dragged head first along the street to Town End, where on reaching the water troughs, he was pushed in and dragged through several times, until he was almost drowned. Afterwards he was conveyed to Dodworth in a cart.

On the succeeding Monday after the ducking, Dowing brought a charge of assault against Thomas Owen, Richard Womack, Michael Prior, George Burland, Lewis Wroe and John Snowball, at the Court convened at Barnsley Town Hall. Dowing said that he went to his lodgings with his brother-in-law to remove his box. When he got into the house Prior and Owen went in and put their fists in his face, Snowball, who was also in the house, said he deserved killing. On going out of the house with the box Dowing was attacked by Snowball, who struck him on the side of the head. Owen pushed Dowing off the box and punched him on the back. On the way to Town End the other defendants assaulted him. At Town End Owen and Burland pushed Dowing into the water troughs. Samuel Cressy, Dowing's brother-in-law, corroborated a portion of Dowing's evidence. He said the person with whom Tom Dowing lived in Somerset Street had blamed him with being the cause of Mrs Downing's death. He told the court that Prior and Owen had struck Dowing over the head, whilst he was in the house. Mr Cressy said that as Dowing was going along the street he was mobbed by a number of men and women. Mr Bury, in addressing the court said:

> ...the assault had arisen out of indignation which reigned in the neighbourhood. The complainant whether rightly or wrongly, was blamed for having caused the death of the woman.

After hearing witnesses for the defence the bench retired for a short time. On their return the chairman said the evidence was conflicting. They had no doubt Tom Dowing was assaulted and put in the troughs, but they were of the opinion that it was done by women. Under the circumstances they had no alternative but to dismiss the case.

A large crowd consisting chiefly of woman had gathered outside the Town Hall. They waited there for over two hours hoping to see Dowing leave. He disappointed them at first. Some time later, as he surreptitiously departed in a cab, he was spotted and left Barnsley amidst the hooting and yelling of the crowd.

❦

SUICIDE AT WENTWORTH CASTLE, 1892
...the water looked so nice and cool that she would like to go in and cool her head.

On the first day of Spring of 1892, Monday 21 March, the body of a young woman was found floating near the bridge crossing the Sepentine in Stainborough Park, which surrounded the palatial mansion Wentworth Castle, home to the Vernon-Wentworth family. The body was that of twenty-one-year-old Hannah Elizabeth Steer, a Sunday School teacher at Stainborough and a member of the choir at the Hood Green Mission, who was learning to be a confectioner at Mrs Birkett's in Church Street, Barnsley. She was the daughter of James Steer, enginewright at Strafford Main Colliery, of Mill House Stainborough. Hannah was highly regarded in the district and her family considered most respectable.

Hannah Steer had been well and strong until 1889 when she

Wentworth Castle, Stainborough. Hannah Steer drowned herself in the serpentine lake situated in the park that surrounds this magnificent stately home.

Robert (Bob) A Dale collection

suffered an attack of St Vitus' dance and rheumatic fever, which confined her to the house for six months. This had weakened her constitution and Hannah was thereafter subject to periods of despondency brought on by severe pains in the head. During Christmas 1891 she was under the care of Dr McCoubrey and orders were given that she was not to be allowed out alone. This was because her sister had told him that Hannah had told her one day when they were crossing the Serpentine that the water looked so nice and cool that she would like to go in a cool her head. Although her health had improved markedly, since that time, until the day of her death she had suffered from headaches, which caused her much distress.

On Sunday 20 March 1892 Hannah attended services at Stainborough in the afternoon and Hood Green in the evening, at which her manner was described as cheerful. Early the following morning she was found dead. The inquest was held at the *Strafford Arms Hotel*, Stainborough on Wednesday 23 March, before Coroner Maitland. Mr W Fisher was fore-man of the jury.

James Steer identified the body as that of his daughter. Despite some health problems Mr Steer said that Hannah had attended well to business walking to and from Barnsley each day and she had no trouble that he knew of. He said he knew of no love affair, no 'sweethearting'. He said that following her illness last Christmas, when she had an attack of rheumatism in the head, which had affected her nerves very much, Dr McCoubrey had attended her for three weeks. As she got well again the only symptoms that remained were periodic pains in the head. On the doctor's instructions the family had watched Hannah carefully while her nerves were so weak. Mr Steer added that they had not noticed any suicidal tendencies lately. She left home to go to business as usual on Monday morning and the next he heard of her she was dead.

Elizabeth Cartwright, widow, of Stainborough Lodge, said she had known the deceased since she was a little girl. She told the inquest that at a quarter to eight on Monday morning she left Stainborough Lodge and began her walk up the Park, as she neared the bridge she saw Hannah step from the side of the bridge across the road onto the grass. She said that Hannah appeared to be watching her. Mrs Cartwright said at the time she did not recognise the young woman as Hannah but did not think it at all unusual to see a young woman there. She said that after she crossed the bridge she went onto the edge of the grass and Hannah went into the trees out of her way. Mrs Cartwright said: 'I didn't think much about it until I saw my little grand-daughter, four-year old, whom I had sent for the milk, and she told me she has seen Hannah Steer on the bridge. Hannah had asked her if she was going for the milk alone and she told her that I was going to follow her.'

Jonathan Moore, joiner, of Stainborough Bottom, said he was going down the road through the Park with a man driving a load of timber, and a lad. They saw a shawl and a black straw hat lying on the battlements of the bridge. The lad had seen Hannah at twenty-past seven and said the items belonged to her. Mr Moore said he noticed footprints on the parapet of the bridge and on looking over saw the deceased lying face down two yards from the bridge, nearly in the middle of the water. Mr Moore said he cut a branch from a tree and drew the body to the side. Mr Moore, assisted by the carter, Thomas Thorpe, Walter Senior and Mrs Cartwright got the body from the water. Hannah was dead but still warm. Mr Moore said he put the dead girl's head lowest down on the bank side, rolled her about and worked her arms and attempted to revive her but this was to no avail. There was a graze on the dead girl's forehead. It appeared that Hannah had stood on the battlements of the bridge, which were 18ft to 25ft above the surface of the water from where she had leaped to her death.

Dr McCoubrey said that if anybody had been there to get her out of the water after the jump, she would have been dead. The coroner said there was no doubt that the pain in the head had acted on her mind until her reason had become unhinged. The jury returned a verdict of 'suicide while suffering from temporary insanity'.

❧❧❧

MAN FOUND GASSED AFTER WIFE LEAVES HIM, KINGSTONE, BARNSLEY, 1947
...there was a gas tube near him and a gas tap had been turned on.

Forty-year-old colliery roadman, Stanley Waite of 33 Cranbrook Street, Kingstone, Barnsley was his usual cheerful self when he went to work for the last time on the night shift on Tuesday 14 October 1947. On Wednesday morning Mr Waite found a note from his wife of thirteen years telling him she had left him.

Stanley Waite's brother-in-law, Albert Gledhill, paper mill labourer, who lived with his sister and her husband in Cranbrook Street, joined Mr Waite and they spent part of Wednesday and all day Thursday looking for his wife. They visited Leicester, where Mrs Waite had connections, thinking she might have gone there but they did not find her.

On their return to Cranbrook Street Stanley Waite was very upset. Albert Gledhill stayed up a while with him, then went to bed after Waite said he was staying downstairs to read a bit. On coming downstairs on Friday morning Mr Gledhill found his brother-in-law lying in the kitchen. There was no smell of gas but there was a gas tube near him and a gas tap had been turned on. He was dead. Waite had left two notes in envelopes.

An inquest was held at Barnsley Town Hall the following morning, Saturday 18 October, before Mr C J Haworth, the West Riding District coroner. In reply to the coroner's questions regarding the state of the marriage and his brother-in-law's general demeanour, Mr Gledhill said that Waite was a very happy man until Wednesday when he found out his wife had left him. He broke down and was very depressed. Mr Gledhill added that in their thirteen years of marriage he had always known his sister and brother-in-law to be happy. The coroner referred to the two notes Waites had left but did not disclose their contents. At the end of the proceedings the coroner recorded a verdict on the body of Stanley Waite of 'suicide while the balance of his mind was disturbed'.

∽∾∽

FAILED TO HANG BUT GASSED HIMSELF INSTEAD, DODWORTH, 1951
… found a rope with a loop attached to the end hanging from a beam at the head of the stairs.

Fifty-six-year-old Dodworth miner Frank Landen spent the evening of Friday 13 April 1951 drinking in one of his usual Dodworth haunts. He returned to his home in Castle View a little before 10pm. Shortly afterwards, his wife, Salina, left to sit at her sick mother-in-law's bedside. She returned home on Saturday morning to find the blinds down and the door locked and, suspecting something was wrong, summoned help from neighbours. Mr Landen's son was sent for and when the house was broken into he found his father lying dead on the floor near the kitchen sink with the flex of the gas pipe leading from a bracket on the wall to his mouth. There was a strong smell of gas present. The police were summoned and some time later Frank Landen's body was taken to the mortuary.

An inquest was held the following week in Dodworth before the West Riding coroner Mr S H B Gill. Alan Landen, an insurance agent, said his father had no financial worries or troubles and had never threatened to take his own life. At 1pm last Saturday he was called to his father's house by a neighbour and had to force entry. When he went into the house there was a strong smell of gas and he found his father dead in the kitchen. Mrs Salina Landen said her husband had not been depressed. For the past ten weeks he had been off work with a series of colds and influenza. She said that when her husband returned home on Friday evening he had had a lot to drink, although he was not drunk. She said that her husband was a very heavy drinker and was ill through drinking.

Police Constable Stanley Ward, stationed at Dodworth, said he was called to the house at 1.25pm. Having seen the deceased in the kitchen, he searched the house and found a rope with a loop attached to the end hanging from a beam at the head of the stairs. The beam was about 5ft 9in from the ground and Constable Ward said he believed Mr Ward had intended to hang himself but on discovering there was insufficient clearance for him to do so, he had gassed himself instead. Constable Ward said he had known the deceased for a long time and on Friday last had had a conversation with him, during which he appeared to be quite cheerful and he knew no reason why he should take his life.

The family doctor, James D Burns, said he had visited Mr Landen regularly during the past few weeks. Dr Burns went on to say that when he was called to the house last Saturday, Mr Landen would have been dead for about eight hours. A post-mortem examination revealed no marks of violence. The cause of death was asphyxia due to inhalation of coal gas.

The coroner said that the deceased had inhaled coal gas and poisoned himself but there was no evidence to show the state of his mind and therefore a verdict that Frank Landen 'inhaled coal gas from a gas jet; there being insufficient evidence to show the state of his mind', was recorded.

HE COULDN'T FACE LIFE WITHOUT HER, 1962
...when he saw his wife leaving the house he seemed to go to pieces.

On Thursday 5 May 1962 there was an inquest on the body of forty-two-year-old Barnsley miner, James Conway, before Mr S H B Gill. Mr Conway was found dead in a van outside his home at 30 Columbia Street, Barnsley.

Mrs Margaret Conway said that her husband, James Conway, had chest trouble and had appeared before the Silicosis Board, two years previously, when he had been granted a ten per cent pneumoconiosis pension. She told the coroner she had been separated from him for about a month and he had gone to live with his sister in a house across the street. Mrs Conway said:

We started having too many rows and we had to separate.

Mrs Conway told the inquest that her husband had threatened to take his life just before the previous Christmas and he had taken two bottles of aspirin but these did not appear to affect him. She said that last Saturday she had gone to stay with relatives in Nuneaton and when she returned home on Easter Monday she learned of her husband's death. She said she had read a letter left by her husband, which indicated he had become severely depressed as a result of their separation. One sentence in the letter read:

...being betrayed by the one judged nearest and dearest.

Mrs Mary Bostwick of 5 Columbia Street, Barnsley, said her brother had been depressed owing to trouble with his wife. She had heard about him taking the aspirins but he had said as late as the Thursday before he died that he would never again attempt to take his life. On Saturday when he saw his wife leaving the house he seemed to go to pieces. That night he told his sister he would like to go and sleep in his own home while his wife was away. Mrs Bostwick said her brother had told her that life without his wife was not worth living. There was no spark left if he could not have her back.

Detective Constable Course said that on Easter Monday he went to Columbia Street and found Mr Conway sitting in a crouched position in the back seat of a small van, outside No.

30. There was a rubber tube leading from the exhaust pipe to the driving cab. He appeared to have been dead for some time.

Dr D G Powell, pathologist, said the cause of death was asphyxia due to carbon monoxide poisoning. The coroner, Mr S H B Gill, said that it was quite obvious that Mr Conway was distressed by his married life and intended to take his own life. A verdict that Mr Conway took his life while in a fit of depression, was recorded.

∽∼∾

FOUND HANGING AT HOME, BARNSLEY, 1965
...he found Dennis hanging on the landing by a leather strap, which was round his neck.

A few days after returning from a holiday at Redcar, thirty-three-year-old, single, colliery ripper, Dennis Reed was found hanging by a leather strap on the landing of his home at 89 Redhill Avenue, Kendray, on Sunday 13 June 1965. An inquest was held at Barnsley on Wednesday 16 June before West Riding District Coroner, Mr S H B Gill.

Dennis Reed's brother-in-law, twenty-eight-year-old miner, Wilfred Holling, of Monk Springs, Worsbrough Dale, said, he was called to the house by the thirteen-year-old sister of the deceased. When he went upstairs he found Dennis hanging on the landing by a leather strap, which was round his neck. He said he couldn't think of any reason why his brother-in-law should take his own life, then added:

He seemed a quiet lad. He had just returned from a holiday at Redcar the previous Tuesday and seemed in good health.

Mrs Alice Ann Reed, wife of Harry Reed and mother of the deceased, said:

Dennis was my eldest son. He never went out of the house last Saturday and was in his room all day apart from coming downstairs for a meal at teatime. He seemed moody...At about eight o'clock on Saturday evening I went upstairs, when I last saw Dennis alive, he was on the landing. I noticed dust on his arms and he was standing underneath the cockloft. He told me to go downstairs.

Mrs Reed also told the coroner that she and her husband did

not get on well together, which upset Dennis.

The following morning, Dennis Reed's youngest sister, who had been staying at a friend's house, came to fetch her clothes. She was going up the stairs when she saw her brother hanging at the top of the stairs and ran for help. Police Constable Gordon Lloyd told the inquest he found Denis Reed hanging by a piece of leather strap attached to an army belt, which had been fastened to a beam in the cockloft. The dead man had a wound about half an inch wide on his chest which could have been caused by a kitchen knife found in his bed.

Coroner's Officer, Detective Constable Stanley Course, said he had spoken to the friend with whom Dennis Reed had recently gone on holiday and the friend had told him that Dennis was his normal self and appeared to have enjoyed the holiday. Pathologist Dr D G Powell, said there was no evidence of organic disease and death was caused by asphyxia due to hanging. The coroner, in summing up said:

> *It seems quite clear from the evidence that this man took his own life, but it is not quite clear why he did it. Maybe it was because his parents were not getting on well together.*

A verdict of 'suicide' was recorded.

ぐ◠◠◡◠◞

POLICE KILLER ENDS HIS OWN LIFE IN A KENDRAY PRESBYTERY'S GARAGE, 1989
The motorcyclist took a handgun from beneath his coat and shot Inspector Codling in the chest; and then, as he stood over him, he shot the injured policeman again, in the head.

A nationwide hunt for a police killer ended in Kendray on the afternoon of Thursday 14 September 1989, after a gunshot was heard. Twelve hours earlier and fifty miles away, across the Pennines, a leather-clad motorcyclist shot two policemen at Birch Service Station on the M62 near Rochdale, Lancashire. Father of five children, Inspector Raymond Codling, aged forty-nine and father of two children, forty-five-year-old Sergeant James Geoffrey Bowden approached a motorcyclist, during a routine patrol. They were stopping vehicles using the service station and checking details during the early hours of 14 September. The motorcyclist took a handgun from beneath his coat and shot Inspector Codling in the chest; and then, as he stood over him, he shot the injured policeman again, in the head. Sergeant Bowden was shot in the leg and grazed on the chest, more serious injury was prevented by the bullet being deflected by Sergeant Bowden's police pocket book. As the gunman fled on his motorcycle, Sergeant Bowden staggered 200 yards to a petrol kiosk to raise the alarm. Colleagues of Inspector Bowden, who were stationed three miles away at Middleton Police Station, were quick to arrive at the scene. They worked with the ambulance crew to try to revive the inspector but he died soon after arrival at hospital. Although seriously injured, Sergeant Bowden was able to tell colleagues what had happened and give a description of the wanted gunman, before he underwent emergency surgery in North Manchester General Hospital. Greater Manchester Police quickly circulated a description of the killer to forces throughout Britain.

At a press conference, Greater Manchester Police's Assistant Chief Constable Jim Patterson said:

This is a dreadful incident. The officers were shot at close range. They were on normal routine patrol, going about their duties. We have lost a very fine policeman indeed. He was an excellent officer and a man with a good future ahead of him. I have seen his wife and stepsons, and they are dreadfully upset. I have done my best to comfort them.

The Chief Constable of Greater Manchester, James Anderton, described the shooting of Inspector Codling as 'a cold-blooded act of extreme violence'. Chairman of the Police Federation, Alan Eastwood said:

I believe parliamentarians must listen to the wishes of the electorate; opinion poll after opinion poll has stated that the majority of people in this country want a return to the death penalty. How many more of my colleagues have to be slaughtered before they come to their senses?

The Prime Minister, Margaret Thatcher, added her voice to a chorus of demands from MPs for the return of capital punishment and claimed it would reduce violent crime. Mrs Thatcher said:

I believe there are some things so horrible that, when there are

*people prepared to take other people's lives in that way, they
should know they may have to forfeit their own.*

Roy Hattersley, Shadow Home Secretary held a different view.
He claimed the restoration of the death penalty would, if
anything, make British society more violent.

As police forces nationwide were hoping for a lead to enable
them to catch the killer, Father John Ashman of St Peter and St
John's Church, situated at the corner of Brinkman Street and
Doncaster Road, Barnsley, received a visit from a leather-clad
biker a little after 11.00am. The man called at the vicarage. He
asked Father John if he was the Catholic priest. Father Ashman
later said:

*A warning bell went in my head. There was something not
quite right about it...We get a lot of wayfarers calling at the
vicarage, either asking for money or a cup of tea. But this was
something different. He was obviously a very trouble man...*

Father John said when he had asked if he was the Catholic
priest:

*I told him I wasn't, and then he asked directions to the nearest
Catholic church...I said it was only down the road. The odd
thing was that he asked me to write down the directions, and
he followed me into the study when I went to get a pen and a
piece of paper... He checked the name of the priest, and I
again gave him explicit instructions on how to get to the
church – and that was it... I was slightly suspicious of the
man. He was rather strange in his behaviour. There was a
certain unease... After he had gone, I immediately rang the
police and, later, officers took a statement. Since then, I have
been frightened... I am very sorry about what has happened.
I just cannot believe this has happened to me.*

Father John called Barnsley Police and told them about his
visitor. Shortly afterwards the motorcyclist arrived at St Joseph's
R C church and school complex, where he asked for Father
Maurice Keenan. Mr David Walsh, headmaster of St Joseph's,
described the motorcyclist as being quietly spoken. Although he
had heard news of the shootings Mr Walsh did not make a
connection. The man was told Father Keenan was away but not
long afterwards staff at the school became suspicious when they

saw him pushing his motorcycle into the small brick-built garage at the side of the Presbytery. Having heard the news about the search for a leather-clad motorcyclist, they contacted the police, at about 11.30am.

There was a significant police presence at St Joseph's within a very short time. The police's first task was to evacuate about 100 children from the nursery and infants schools to Ted Johnson's car salesrooms a safe distance away. A teacher at the school. Carol Turner, told the *Barnsley Chronicle*:

> *The children and staff had lunch in the school but soon afterwards police arrived and said it would be dangerous to stay. They had already got an offer from Ted Johnson's to accommodate the children and we all went up there. The garage staff were very good in helping us to keep the children occupied.*

The children's evacuation coincided with the arrival of a small contingent of armed police, wearing flak jackets. At 1.06pm a single gunshot was heard coming from the garage. Ninety-minutes later, after more armed officers had arrived, police searched the house and garage and found the dead man, dressed in black motorcycle leathers, lying in a pool of blood, a handgun at his side.

The Barnsley Division deputy commander, Superintendent Terry Swann, in commenting about police being summoned to St Joseph's said:

> *In view of the incident in Greater Manchester we immediately responded and from the outset a small contingent of armed officers went to the house and contained the immediate area.*

The dead man was identified as forty-two-year-old Anthony Kenneth Hughes.

Mr Walter Krei, aged sixty-two, stepfather of Anthony Hughes, with whom Hughes shared a home in Bideford Drive, Baguley, South Manchester, said that his stepson had spoken recently of taking revenge on the police force which had arrested him several times. During Hughes' long criminal career, since 1968 he had been sentenced to twenty-three years' imprisonment, for crimes including rape, armed robbery and the impersonation of a police officer. With remissions he had spent fifteen years in jail. Mr Krei said that his stepson had vowed never to return to prison and added:

He was talking about revenge and saying the police had beaten him up badly when he was in prison. Last week he said to me, "I hope everything will be alright. Wish me luck and say prayers for me." Revenge was always on his mind. He had spent so many years in prison. When I saw him the week before the killing he said he had had enough.

Tests on the 9mm handgun found beside Hughes' body confirmed it was the same weapon used to kill Inspector Codling and wound Sergeant Bowden. The gun had been stolen about two years previously from the car of a member of the Diggle Gun Club near Oldham. Anthony Hughes began his first stretch in prison in 1968, when he was sentenced to six years imprisonment for robbery with violence. Within a few days of his release in March 1972, he committed burglaries and two armed robberies at a sub-post office and garage. He received a ten-year sentence, of which he served seven years, being released in March 1979. Two weeks later, dressed in a police uniform he raped a teenager at knifepoint and committed a series of other offences. He received a seven years sentence at Mold Crown Court in Clwyd, for rape, burglary, theft and impersonating a police officer. At the time of the shooting Hughes was being sought for questioning in connection with three armed robberies in the Manchester area.

Tributes were paid to the Inspector Codling and to the wounded Sergeant Bowden. Their commanding officer at Middleton, Superintendent Brian Mottram said:

They were first class individuals of whom you were proud and pleased to know.

Inspector Codling had been married twice and had three children by his first wife. He and his second wife, Linda would have celebrated their tenth wedding anniversary the following month. One of his two stepsons, twenty-year-old Lincoln Codling, at the family home in Schoolside Road, Rhodes, Middleton, said:

He had the respect not only of colleagues but of the people he arrested – he was a gentleman copper. We had all talked about the dangers of his job but you never think it will happen to you.

The dead policeman's other stepson, Anthony, aged twenty-three said:

My dad said the job was getting harder.

To which Lincoln Codling added:

He probably meant having to face men with guns, armed only with truncheons.

Sergeant Bowden's wife, Jennifer, in referring to the pocket book, which deflected the bullet said:

The chest pocket of his uniform probably saved his life.

Mrs Bowden visited Inspector Codling's widow. Afterwards she said:

It could easily have been the other way round and I could have lost Jim. I am proud of what he did.

Chapter 4

Suspicious Deaths, 1865–1948

MYSTERIOUS DEATH IN BARNSLEY, 1865
It bore no external marks of violence.

On the afternoon of Thursday 30 March 1865, Michael Hart of Silver Street, Barnsley, who was employed as a porter with Mr Fox, wine and spirit merchant of Church Street, was directed to clean out a water tank on the top storey of the Central Chambers, Barnsley. The Central Chambers were occupied as public offices, and a suite on the ground floor had been occupied for the previous four months by Joseph Nottingham, who also occupied a bedroom situated on the top floor, adjacent to the water system. A woman named Ellen Briggs, aged about thirty, was employed to clean the premises. Mr Hart set to work and after taking out some water he found a bundle, which having been opened proved to be the body of a tiny child in a state of putrefaction. It was wrapped in an apron, the strings of which were passed around the child's neck. He took the child's body to the police station.

The following day, Friday 31 March, an inquest was held at the *Westgate Tavern*, Barnsley, before Thomas Taylor, Esq, on the body of an unknown infant male. Neither Mr Hart, Mr Nottingham or Ellen Briggs could throw any light as to how the child's body came to be in the water tank. Mr William Stawman, surgeon, of Barnsley, examined the body at the police station. He gave evidence to the effect that the body was in a state of advance decomposition. The navel string had evidently not been separated by a surgeon or midwife; and was not tied, but had apparently been torn. The body was that of a perfectly developed male child. It bore no external marks of violence. During the post-mortem examination, Mr Stawman said he discovered that nothing had been taken into the stomach; and all the organs were greatly congested, particularly on the right side. Mr Stawman said from the appearances observed, he would not say positively that the deceased had been born alive, but was of the opinion that it was. He could not state from the decomposed state of the lungs whether it had breathed, but thought it had. Mr Stawman also said that the baby boy had died shortly after birth and he concluded by the fact that the naval string had not been tied, there had been not intention of preserving the child's life, whether it were born alive or not; and that it had died of suffocation. Mr Stawman concluded his evidence by saying he believed the child had been dead between two to five weeks. As there was no further evidence to be presented, the jury returned an open verdict of 'found dead'.

꽁뎒

A MONK BRETTON MYSTERY, 1899/1900
...he had expressed his intention to end his life or to flee the country.

The body of twenty-eight-year-old glassblower Richard Thomas Wormald of Littleworth, Monk Bretton, was discovered in Barnsley Canal on Tuesday 2 January 1900 between Cliffe Bridge and Littleworth. Richard Wormald disappeared on the night of Tuesday 28 November 1899. He was last seen alive about 10.15pm, when he left by the back door of the *Hope Inn*, Cliffe Bridge, to set off for home along the canal bank. It was a dark night. Next day his corduroy cap was found in the water. His disappearance followed within a short time of him being acquitted on a charge of wilful murder. Although the canal had been dragged several times over in the vicinity of where the body was eventually found and hope had been abandoned of ever finding it, surprisingly, even after five weeks when it floated to the surface the corpse was sufficiently well preserved to enable the remains to be positively identified by his uncle, John Beaumont, a miner of 18 Littleworth, with whom the deceased man lived.

    The inquest on the body of Richard Thomas Wormald was held before the Coroner, Mr P P Maitland, at the *Sun Inn*, Monk Bretton on the evening the body was found. By coincidence, Mr Maitland had presided at the inquest on the body of Anne Whitehead at the *Norman Inn*, the previous April, the woman of whose murder Richard Maitland had been accused. On the morning of Sunday 2 April 1899, Alfred Scales of Rock Crescent found the dead body of Anne

A present day view of the Hope Inn, *Cliffe Bridge.* The Author

An Edwardian view of the canal at Monk Bretton. Chris Sharp of Old Barnsley

Whitehead of Albert Street, Barnsley at the entrance to Cliffe Quarry, Monk Bretton. Dr McSweeney's evidence indicated that the woman had been partially strangled and had died from shock. The jury returned a verdict of 'Wilful murder by person or persons unknown.' Investigations led to the arrest of Thomas Wormald, as he was the last person to have been seen with her on Saturday night, a few hours before her body had been found. The following week he was taken before magistrates at the West Riding Court at Barnsley and committed for trial on the capital charge of murder, at Leeds Assizes, where at the suggestion of the judges the grand jury threw out the charge and Wormald was set free. After this ordeal it was said of him he was happy and contented as usual at home but amongst his friends he had expressed his intention to end his life or to flee the country.

Thomas Wormald had lived with his uncle John for fourteen years, when as a boy he had arrived at the door and asked if he could stay. When Mr Beaumont had asked his nephew: 'Will it be alright for your father?' Thomas replied: 'Never mind my father, my father is not a father to me.' Mr Beaumont told the inquest that his brother-in-law lived in Worsbrough Dale with another of his sons and that since Thomas had resided with him,

The Sun Inn, *Monk Bretton, where the inquest on the body of Richard Wormald was held on Tuesday 2 January 1900*

his father had never owned him as a son. Mr Beaumont told the coroner:

We had a bit of bother a while since, when he was blamed...I never saw any difference in him until about three weeks or a month ago [meaning the last three weeks of his life], *when he seemed to be a lot steadier and to keep better hours. I thought he was going to turn over and be a right good lad again...He had been no ways 'irregular,' but had a sup of beer. Then he took less beer and I never saw him jollier than he was on Monday night* [November 27]...*He had never shown any symptoms of being depressed and never done anything to make me think he would commit suicide. I never heard him say he was tired of life. He was too fond of himself for that. Too fond of life.*

When the coroner asked Mr Beaumont if he had found a letter or anything of that kind, he replied:

No, nothing, except his Union card which was found in his pocket, and 7s. 9d.

Alfred North Wiseman, landlord of the *Hope Inn,* said Richard Wormald had been in the habit of coming to his house as a customer. On the morning of the day he had disappeared Richard Wormald had accompanied him to Pontefract to buy some pigs. They had returned to the *Hope Inn* between seven and eight o'clock that evening. Afterwards they had dined and at about a quarter past ten Richard had left by the back door. He had had a drink but was quite sober.

George Binns of Field Lane, Stairfoot, boatman, said on the afternoon of Tuesday 2 January 1900 he was on his boat between Cliffe Bridge and Littleworth when he saw a body floating on its side, with the hair showing out of the water about 200 yards from Cliffe Bridge. He got out of his boat and brought the body to the canal bank. When asked by the coroner how the body could have remained in the canal for so long without being discovered, Mr Binns replied that there were several holes near that place where the water varied from between 6ft to 9ft deep. Another witness, Ann Peaker of Ann's Terrace, said there were no marks of violence on the body. Following their deliberations the jury returned a verdict of 'found drowned without mark of violence'.

OPEN VERDICT ON EXHUMED CHILDREN, DODWORTH, 1948
I think there has been great neglect in the hospital and on the local doctor's part.

Following accusations by the family of three Silkstone children that their deaths were suspicious their bodies were exhumed and examined and an inquest was opened and adjourned on 16 March 1948, resumed and again adjourned on 20 April in view of proceedings that were taking place in another court and that case having now been completed, the inquest on the children's bodies was finally resumed on Thursday 29 July before Coroner S H B Gill on the exhumed bodies of the three children of bus conductor Edward Roy Wright and his wife Gwendoline, of Pack Horse Green, Silkstone; these being: John Edward Francis, aged five, who died in 1944, Jean Alice, aged four, who died in March 1946 and Kathleen Mary, aged two, who died in September 1946.

In his evidence, pathologist, Professor P L Sutherland said he undertook post-mortem examinations on the bodies of the three children but owing to putrefaction was unable to determine the cause of death. The death certificates stated in each case that the children died of pneumonia and in two cases post epileptic coma also appeared on the certificates.

The coroner asked the children's father, Edward Wright, if he would like to ask any questions. Mr Francis replied in the affirmative and, after stating all three children had died in hospital said:

> *Where were the hospital in allowing three children to die without making any investigations? Three healthy well developed children and two of them die within a matter of months, they never had a convulsion let alone epilepsy.*

The coroner answered Mr Wright:

> *I do not see how Professor Sutherland can answer that question. He says they all appeared to be very well-nourished children.*

Mr Wright then said:

I think there has been great neglect in the hospital and on the local doctor's part.

The Director of the Forensic Laboratory at Wakefield, Lewis Charles Nickolls, who examined the internal organs of all three children said in the case of Wright he found definite, positive, chemical reaction of a barbiturate substance, which led him to believe there had been barbitone in the body. Mr Nickolls went on to say:

But I am not in a position to state that as a definite scientific fact.

Mr Nickolls then told the inquest that he found no trace of barbitone in the bodies of either John or Kathleen Wright.

When the coroner asked Mr Nickolls,

You cannot express any opinion to the cause of death?

Mr Nickolls replied:

None at all.

The coroner in addressing the jury said that taking the medical evidence into account the only safe verdict was to find that the cause of the children's death was not shown. Open verdicts were returned and recorded on the bodies of all three children.

CHAPTER 5

A Stabbing, Silkstone Common, 1854

My opinion is that the wounding of the colon caused his death, and no treatment whatever could have saved him.

On Saturday 31 August 1854, an inquest was opened on the body of George Turton, at the *Bunch of Roses*, Silkstone Common, kept by Mr W Tattershall. On Monday 14 August, the feast-day at Silkstone, a fight had taken place, during which George Turton had received stab wounds which had resulted in his death. Two days after the affray in which he was injured, George Turton made a deposition in the presence of John Spencer Stanhope, Esq, magistrate, as follows:

> *I am a miner, and was 29 years of age last April. I am not married. I remember last Monday night, August 14th. I was at this house, Mr Tattershall's [the* Bunch of Roses]. *I was in company with my brother, John Lister, John Howden, James Pinder, Joseph Garnett and William Garnett. There were many more in the public-house, but not when we went out. I heard a bit of a scuffle at the other house (John Gaunt's), opposite to this house. I went to it, and went into Gaunt's to ask my father if he was ready to go home. When I got there they were just knocking Isaac Can down. It was John Bower. I told him he should not do that with an old man. He said, 'I will do the same by you if you do not hold your noise.' I said, 'I think you will not.' I saw they were turning out, and I went back again. When I got out John Bower and his sons, and other two young men were up the road. I was going across the road to the Garnetts; Bower shouted out and asked what I wanted. It was William Bower that called out. I said I wanted anything I could get. William Bower answered, 'Come to me and I will give you what you will get.' When I got up to Bower, I said, 'Now I have come.' Bower said, 'Thou has come and thou ar't going to have something before thou goes back.' William Bower said this. I replied, 'Who will give it to me?' and Bower said,*

'He.' John Bower said if he (William Bower) could not, he (John) could. I said, 'Neither of you can if fair play is shown.' Directly Bill and me started fighting. Bill struck first and caught me over my left cheek. We scuffled until I got him down. It was Bill I had down. When we were down Bower's father and the youngest son fell on the top of us and began punching. I was kicked, and before I could get up a knife came into me. It was in my arm the first time. I was going away as well as I could, and the youngest brother, Bower, and father got me again. They knocked me down. I was getting up and a knife went into my belly. It was the youngest brother that sent the knife into me. I set off as well as I could, and they ran after me, and cut me on my thigh just before I got to the door. The youngest brother (Bower) did this. I got into this house and I did not see them again. This is all. I was as sober as I am now. I have known the Bowers for about twelve months. It was the youngest son who made all the wounds. I was stuck in the belly twice by the younger son. It was nearly dark. I don't know much about the youngest son. None of the other four men stabbed me. I saw the youngest son have something in his hand, but I do not know what. I know the youngest son by his father saying, 'I will not have either of my lads hurt.' I have seen the youngest son once or twice before. I am now quite sensible, and aware of my dangerous situation. I hope I shall get better. I think I shall get better. I am attended by two surgeons. I was stripped when I was fighting. There were about eight or nine fighting. I did not tell who had cut me. I see five men in this room. I know some of them. I know John Bower, William Bower, and the other Bower. The last is the youngest. I do not know the other two by name. I have seen them before they were there. I hope to recover but I am aware I am in danger. The person who stabbed me had a blue slop on.

George Turton died in the early hours of Saturday 31 August. An inquest was held that night at the *Bunch of Roses*, where he had breathed his last and close to the spot where he had been stabbed.

James Pinder, of Silkstone Common, miner, said:

I know George Turton. I saw him on 14th of August in this chamber at about half-past ten at night. He was dancing with a young woman. I saw him a quarter of an hour after this. I *saw him out of doors, just up the road. He was talking to William Bower. There were some other men there, and when I got up to them they began fighting. I saw George Turton strike William Bower. They struggled together, and both fell on the side of the road. William Bower's wife was standing by screaming. She called out 'Oh, dear! Oh, dear!' I said, 'I will part them.' She said, 'Do, lad.' George had his arm under Bower's neck, and when they got up he began to punch William Bower. John Howden, of Silkstone, came up. I said, 'John, let's part them,' and we lifted George off William. We brought George Turton to Tattershall's house corner. John Bower then caught up and said, 'What's up here?' I said, 'Turton and Bower have been fighting.' He swore at me and hit me over the head with his fist, and knocked me against the wall. After this William Beverley said, 'Turton has got struck.' I went into the house, and saw Turton laid on two chairs in the kitchen. Turton had his clothes off, Bower had not. I saw John Bower and Griffith Bower amongst the crowd.*

John Howden of Silkstone, miner, said:

I saw George Turton on Monday night, the 14th August, about eleven o'clock. On having a race up the road, I heard George Turton quarrelling with somebody , but there was so many I could not tell who it was with. I did not think there was going to be any fighting, for he began putting his clothes on. Shortly after this, George Turton and William Bower began fighting against Tattershall's garden wall. When I got to them they were both laid upon the ground. I lifted Turton up. Bower went with Joseph Garnett and when he got to the middle of the road he held up his fist and said, 'See I can make it cut like a knife.' Directly afterwards I saw Turton run round the crowd twice and give a scream, I then lost him. There was no one near him when he screamed. I went into the house with John Turton, and saw deceased laid on a chair.

Mr William Ellis of Silkstone, surgeon, said:

I have known Turton from infancy. He was injured on the evening of the 14th August; I saw him about half-past twelve o'clock on the morning of the 15th. I was called up by his father; when I arrived here I fund him in the kitchen, undressed except [for] his trousers and stockings. He was very faint and sick. I ordered him to bed in this house. On examining him externally I found a wound about one inch above the navel, in length about an inch and a half in the external orifice, and penetrating through the integuments, wounding the omentum, which covers the bowels. The lower orifice of the wound was not more than one-half inch in length, through which a portion of the omentum protruded about the size of a pigeon's egg. This was found so congested that it was necessary to cut it off. There was another incised wound, one inch in length, about 2½ below the right side of the navel, also penetrating the cavity of the abdomen and wounding the colon to the extent of an inch. There was another incised wound on the upper right arm, near the shoulder, lacerating the muscles to the depth of 1½ inch in the centre of the wound, and about five inches in length. I found a fourth wound on the upper portion of the right thigh, 1½ inch in length and nearly two inches in depth. I treated him in the ordinary way and considered him in great danger. I have visited him three or four times a day ever since and have used all approved methods usual in such cases. I have always considered him in great danger, and expected him to die much sooner. I had given him up two or three times. At last he died from exhaustion and effusion in the peritoneum. I visited him up to eleven o'clock last night and he died at five o'clock this morning.

Following the death of George Turton on Saturday morning, a post-mortem examination of his body was conducted that afternoon by the surgeon who had attended him, assisted by Mr Wainwright, a surgeon from Barnsley. Mr Ellis described the examination of Turton's remains:

On opening the chest we found the lungs and heart perfectly healthy. We next examined the cavity of the abdomen and found the peritoneum and omentum in a gangrenous state, and the portion of the colon before named wounded to the extent of an inch, through which opening the contents of the bowels had escaped., which produced inflammation and death. It was impossible for him to get better with such a wound. My opinion is that the wounding of the colon caused his death, and no treatment whatever could have saved him. I consider it astonishing that he has lived so long. The other wounds had nothing to do with his death. I found all the wounds narrower at the bottom than at the external orifice, and they appeared to have been caused by some sharp instrument. A common pocket-knife would produce such wounds.

Mr Wainwright, on being examined by the coroner confirmed the evidence of Mr Ellis in every particular. He said he considered death to have been as a result of the rent in the bowels.

John Lister, miner, of Higham, said:

> *I have known the deceased since his birth, he is my half brother, and is 29 years of age, and by trade a miner. I saw him on Monday the 14th, about half-past ten, in this house. He was dancing when I came in, and he asked me to drink with him. He went down stairs a little before eleven o'clock. When I saw him again he was fighting with William Bower; this was directly after he went down stairs. I went down, and as soon as I got there my father said 'What are you three or four going at him for?' When I heard this I went up to them, about eight or ten yards up the road. He was on the floor with William Bower. I said, 'George, give up or else they'll kill thee.' He made no answer but came away to this house. I saw in the road James Pinder, Joseph Garnett, John Holden and William Garnett. My brother was on the top of William Bower. While I was standing Old Bower came up and struck me on the eye and side of the head with something sharp. The Bowers were all tipsy. After John Bower struck me he went from me to Joseph Garnett. I then came away; I was quite sober; having had only one glass of ale. I did not see the Bowers after this. When I first got up I saw my father pull Griffith Bower away. I knew it was Griffith because I had been with him in this house. There was no quarrelling before they went out. I cannot state which of them went out first. I have known the Bowers about nine months.*

William Tattershall, landlord of the *Bunch of Roses,* said that for the first time that evening on the 14 August he saw George Turton in his house at about seven o'clock. Later, at about eleven o'clock, he saw him again. He was standing at the bar in his shirt sleeves talking to Joseph Garnett. There was some noise in Garnett's house opposite and they went to the door to see what was happening. When Mr Tattershall followed them he saw George Turton was in the middle of the road and heard him shout, 'Tally ho!' Mr Tattershall then said:

I went into my bar and returned to the door again in about five minutes, and heard a noise a short distance up the road.

On Thursday 6 December 1854, Griffith Bower appeared at York Assizes before Mr Justice Crowder, indicted with the manslaughter of George Turton. Mr Pickering and Mr Johnston prosecuted. Mr Overbend defended. With overwhelming witness evidence against him, the jury found Bower guilty of manslaughter and Mr Justice Crowder sentenced him to fifteen years' transportation.

Silkstone Common. The Bunch of Roses *is the first building on the right of the photograph, with steps leading to the front door.*

CHAPTER 6

Fatal Fight at the *Shepherd's Rest,* Barnsley, 1864

...found him dead, in exactly the same position she had left him.

On Wednesday 29 June 1864 Thomas Jackson, known to some as Flycatcher, and Jonathan Fitton, a tailor, were drinking in the *Shepherd's Rest*, a public house in Heelis Street, Barnsley, kept by Daniel Lidgett. During the lengthy drinking session a quarrel broke out between the two men and Fitton got up to fight Jackson several times before a tussle eventually occurred in the passage, after which Fitton went home, where he soon died.

An inquest on the body of thirty-year-old Jonathan Fitton was held at the *Neptune* in New Street, Barnsley before the coroner, Thomas Taylor, Esq, on Saturday 2 July. The jury having first been taken to view the body, which had been taken to the *Shepherd's Rest*, the inquest was opened.

The deceased's widow, Hannah Fitton, said that her husband had been in the habit of repeatedly getting drunk of late and that he had gone out at about half-past one on Wednesday afternoon. At about four o'clock she had gone to look for him and eventually found her husband in the *Shepherd's Rest* in the company of Thomas Jackson. When she told him his tea was ready, her husband replied he did not want any tea and she returned home. She went back to the public house at about seven o'clock and found Jackson and her husband quarrelling. Jackson told Fitton that he would go out and fight him if he had not had enough in fighting a man a week before he would now give him enough. Both men having calmed down, Hannah Fitton again went home only to return to the public house an hour later. There she discovered her husband with his coat off, apparently ready to fight. Fitton told his wife to go home, which she did. A while later she went out to deliver some clothes and when she came back she found her husband lying down on the floor in front of the hearth, which in a drunken condition he habitually did.

On seeing his wife Fitton put his hand to his head and said:

Come lass, let's go home.

Hannah Fitton replied:

We are at home.

When she saw tears running down her husband's face, Hannah asked:

Has he hurt thee?

He replied:

Yes.

A late Victorian view of New Street, Barnsley, where the inquest on the body of James Fitton was held at the Neptune *public house on Saturday 2 July 1864.*

Chris Sharp of Old Barnsley

When she asked him where, he replied: 'His head.' Her husband never uttered a word again. She went to bed at about a quarter-past eleven and left him in what she thought was a sound sleep. At about one o'clock the following morning she went downstairs to see how he was and found him dead, in exactly the same position she had left him.

Mr John Blackburn, surgeon, stated that in conjunction with Dr Sadler he had made a post-mortem examination of the body. He had first been called out at about four o'clock on Thursday morning when he found the deceased man lying before the hearth, fully clothed and in a state of considerable rigor mortis. The *Barnsley Chronicle* reported a full transcript of the medical evidence, part of which said:

> *On examining the head, and having the scalp reflected much ecchymosis was found upon the left temple, and over the occiput, or back of the head. There were several bruises and a partially healed wound on the back of the left hand. On the skull-cap being removed, a large clot of blood was found between the bone and the* dura mater, *with a flattening of the brain corresponding to the 'clot.' On the* dura mater *being still further deflected a fracture of the skull was found, radiating in three directions from the right temporal bone. The skull-cap had previously been sawn through with the greatest care , and was afterwards lifted off with the fingers with the same precaution, so that no injury to the bone could arise from the examination. The fracture extended through and above the sawn portion, thus showing that the fracture existed before the skull was opened. The brain was healthy, as were all the organs of the body except the left kidney, which was larger than the right one and much congested...*

Mr Blackburn said that in his opinion the cause of death was a fracture to the right side of the skull, rupturing the artery and producing an effusion of blood on the brain. Such an injury might result from a blow or a fall, most probably the latter.

A little girl named Harriet Smeaton, of John Street, Wilson's Piece, had been sitting on the doorstep of the *Shepherd's Rest* when she saw Jackson struggling with Fitton in the passage. She told the inquest that she saw Jackson 'braying' Fitton's head on the floor and she had heard Jackson saying he would 'split his skull as near as he dared'.

Daniel Lidgett, landlord of the *Shepherd's Rest* said that on

Tuesday 28 June he was in conversation with Jonathan Fitton. Fitton had told him that a short time before he had had a fight with someone and he had suffered much in his head and chest ever since. He said that the following day when an argument broke out between Fitton and Jackson in his house, despite his efforts to reconcile them they ultimately began to fight and during a struggle in the passage Fitton was thrown down and the back of his head struck the stone floor. He said Fitton did not complain of receiving any injury befor he had left his house. Mr Lidgett added the first he knew that Fitton had been injured was when he was told of his death the following morning.

The surgeon, Mr Blackburn, expressed the opinion that Fitton's death was as a result of the injuries he had received on Wednesday 29 June as the fracture was recent and could not have been inflicted a week before. In his summing up the coroner told the jury that if they considered that Jonathan Fitton's death had been caused or hastened by the injuries he sustained on Wednesday night then they should return a verdict of manslaughter against Thomas Jackson, which after fifteen minutes deliberation they did. Thomas Jackson was taken into custody and subsequently sent for trial at the West Riding Assizes.

Thomas Jackson appeared at the West Riding Assizes before Mr Justice Keating on Saturday 20 August, charged with the manslaughter of Jonathan Fitton. Mr V Black prosecuted. Jackson was defended by Mr Waddy. The prisoner at first pleaded 'not guilty' but afterwards changed his plea to 'guilty'. After hearing the evidence the jury found Jackson guilty but recommended him for mercy. Mr Justice Keating said that he should consider the jury's recommendation and he did not think the case was one calling for a very severe punishment, as the deceased had apparently been the aggressor. Bearing that in mind the judge decided to pass a very light sentence on the prisoner. Jackson was sentenced to one month imprisonment with hard labour, to date from the opening of the court.

CHAPTER 7

The Slaying of Norfolk Tom, Platts Common, 1856

...Wood had been knocking about all day, wanting to fight somebody.

On Saturday 1 March 1856 an inquest was held at the *Strafford Arms Inn,* Hoyland, before T Badger, coroner and what the *Barnsley Times* described as a highly respectable jury (of which R C Webster of Hoyland Hall was foreman). The inquest was convened on the body of Thomas Wood, whose death resulted from injuries inflicted by his employer, Henry Eastwood at the *Pheasant Ale House,* Platts Common, kept by Joseph Turner, on the previous Thursday.

Henry Eastwood, aged thirty-one, was present in custody and was represented by Mr Tyas of Barnsley. The first witness to be examined was the dead man's step-father, John Norfolk, who identified the body as that of his twenty-three-year-old stepson, Thomas Wood, late of Worsbrough Dale, a shoemaker by trade, but lately working as a mason's labourer in the employ of the prisoner, Eastwood. Mr Norfolk added that Mr Wood was sometimes called 'Norfolk Tom', on account of himself having married the dead man's mother.

Thomas Clarke, stonemason, of Blacker Hill, in his evidence said that he was at the *Pheasant Ale House* on the day the tragedy occurred, between eleven and twelve o'clock, when the deceased came in with another man. About half an hour later Eastwood arrived. Mr Clarke said that shortly after Eastwood's arrival, he saw the deceased man, Thomas Wood, hit an elderly person named Samuel Smith, a joiner, several times on the head. Eastwood saw him do this and told Wood to sit down. It transpired that Wood had been 'knocking about all day', wanting to fight somebody. Evidently still intent on achieving his aim to have a fight, Mr Clarke said that at about two o'clock Wood got up to fight Eastwood, having already stripped three times for that purpose beforehand. At one point Wood had gone outside and, having returned, Eastwood told him that if he did not sit down and behave himself he would make him. Eastwood, however, did not want to fight and pushed Wood down on to the form, and told him to sit down and be quiet. Wood got up off the form and struck Eastwood, who was seated, over the face. Eastwood stood up, seized Wood by the hair with his left hand and in the tussle that followed struck him four times over the face with his right hand, whilst Wood's head was against the stone mantelpiece. Blood poured from a wound opened at the back of Wood's head. Eastwood did not restrain himself when inflicting the blows and appeared to strike Wood as hard as he could. The landlord came in and, catching hold of Eastwood, pulled him backwards as he was striking Wood. Eastwood then let go of Wood, who promptly fell on the floor as Eastwood kicked out twice at him. The first kick missed but the second struck Wood on the left breast. However, Mr Clarke's evidence was slightly at variance with that given by Samuel Smith, a carpenter, of Hemingfield. Mr Smith corroborated the time that

The Strafford Arms Inn, *Hoyland, where the inquest on the body of Norfolk Tom was held.* Sandra Hague

the events occurred and commented that Eastwood did not seem to be tipsy, while Wood appeared to be very fresh. He said that when he saw Wood hit the old man he had called out: 'Don't strike an old man!' to which Wood replied: 'Blast your old eyes, I'll drive your head off.' At which point Mr Smith said he sat down. James Wood (no relation to the deceased man), miner, who lodged at the *Pheasant Ale House*, gave his account of the events which were corroborated by John Camm of Jump and Joseph Dickenson, stonemason, of Upper Hoyland. The general consensus of opinion among witnesses was that Eastwood, who had only consumed four pints of ale, was quite sober, whereas Wood was very drunk. James Wood, assisted by the landlady, picked Thomas Wood up and put him in a chair. The injured man was quite insensible and did not speak again. Medical assistance was sent for.

A surgeon, Mr Robert Adamson, arrived at the *Pheasant Ale House* a little after three o'clock. He found Thomas Wood seated in a chair in a corner of the bar, supported by two men. Mr Adamson on realising the serious nature of Wood's injuries ordered that he be taken upstairs. He told the inquest that he had, after only a brief examination, concluded that Wood, who was breathing with considerable difficulty, was a dying man. Mr Adamson added that Wood smelled strongly of drink. He applied warmth to try and revive Wood but this was to no avail as he soon expired. Regarding the extent of Wood's injuries, the *Barnsley Times* reported that Mr Adamson said that he:

> ...*assisted by Mr. Booth* [presumably Dr Booth, of the recently built Netherfield House, Hoyland] *and Mr Wainwright, of Barnsley, had made a post-mortem examination of the body, and found externally a blackened contusion over the right eye, and contusion of the left side of the nose and upper lip. On examining the head* [they] *found a small wound on the back part of it, slightly penetrating the integuments; there were also some slight bruises on the shins. On removing the scalp they found an effusion of blood over the right parietal bone, corresponding internally with the separation of the dura mater (or covering of the brain), and about two or three ounces of coagulated blood effused between the dura mater and the brain, caused by the rupture of the middle meningeal artery; the brain was otherwise healthy, with the exception of some old adhesions between the*

arachnoid membrane and the dura mater. The deceased had evidently suffered from epilepsy, and had been subject to fits. The whole of the internal organs were perfectly healthy...the man died from an effusion of blood in the right hemisphere of the brain, causing compression, and produced by a severe blow or fall. There was no fracture or depression of the skull, which was of extraordinary thinness, not being thicker than a sheet of ordinary brown paper...

Mr Wainwright said that he was perfectly satisfied that the effusion of blood did not arise from excitement but from violence.

The coroner, Mr Badger, then addressed the jury. He told them that he regretted the drinking customs of the people should so often lead to such crimes of violence. It was, however, to the credit of the old and established houses (one presumes he meant such as the *Strafford Arms Inn* and older establishments in the locality serving beer, porter, cider, wines and spirits) that these fatal affrays mostly occurred in beer houses. Mr Badger

Platts Common. The Pheasant Ale House *was situated about one hundred yards down the road which goes off to the left, the corner of which can be seen behind the man with the bowler hat in the left foreground.* Chris Sharp of Old Barnsley

expressed his opinion that the establishment of these beer houses (which served only beer or ale, which the drink is often referred to as. Such establishments be more often frequented by the lower classes) had done more to demoralise the working man than almost anything else. He said he would be glad to see the day on which they would all be swept away. Mr Badger concluded by saying that it was for the jury to decide how Thomas Wood died and if they believed the evidence given by witnesses there could be little doubt that his death had resulted from violence. After a short break the coroner's jury returned a verdict of manslaughter against Henry Eastwood and he was committed to York to stand trial at the Spring Assizes.

At the Yorkshire Spring Assizes a fortnight later, Henry Eastwood appeared on a charge of manslaughter. The defence argued that the deceased man, Thomas Wood, was the aggressor and that the prisoner used no more violence than was necessary to protect himself. The defence further argued that Eastwood had used no offensive weapon and taking all the circumstances of the case into account the prisoner was not legally guilty of any offence. The jury agreed with the defence counsel and Henry Eastwood was found not guilty and set at liberty.

Hoyland Hall, the home of R C Webster, Esq, who was foreman of the jury at the inquest. Walkers Newsagents collection

CHAPTER 8

Attempted Murder and Suicide, Barnsley, 1892

...Brocksom went to Messrs Reynolds and Wadsworth, ironmongers in Church Street. There he purchased from Albert Bright a six chambered revolver and a box of fifty ball cartridges.

On Monday 11 March 1892, appearing in the dock at Barnsley Court House before Mr John Dyson (Chairman) and Mr E Lancaster, was twenty-six-year-old Frederick William Brocksom, baker, of Granville Street, situated near the Old Reservoir, Huddersfield Road, Barnsley. He was charged with having on 26 March shot at his wife Martha, with the intention of murdering her and on the same day attempting to commit suicide by slitting his throat. Mr Catterall prosecuted and Mr John Carrington defended.

The prisoner had been brought from Beckett Hospital that morning and was allowed to sit during the proceedings. Haggard looking, blue-eyed and frequently giving way to tears, Brocksom was evidently in an extremely weak state. He appeared to view his condition very seriously, which was in complete contrast to his wife who did not seem at all moved and maintained a most cool and collected demeanour throughout. Superintendent Kane stated the nature of the charges against the prisoner.

The prisoner and his wife were married in July 1890 at Earlsheaton near Dewsbury. They had lived there until June 1891 when they moved to Barnsley. They had no children but Martha Brocksom was a widow when she married him and had two children from her previous marriage. Brocksom was by occupation a baker and he obtained a position at the Co-operative stores near Summer Lane Station in Barnsley.

At lunchtime on Friday 25 March, acting on information she had received, Martha Brocksom asked her husband if he was going to leave his work permanently the next day, to which he did not give a direct reply but his manner suggested that this was indeed his intention. During their short marriage Frederick Brocksom had already spent six months unemployed resulting in his wife having to sell furniture and other valuables to support them. Martha told him that she would not live with him any longer and she would not have her house sold up (meaning the furnishings and chattels she had brought with her from her first marriage). She said she would leave him and take the two

Church Street, Barnsley. Messrs Reynolds and Wadsworth, the ironmongers, situated at No. 18, was where Frederick Brocksom purchased a six-chambered revolver and fifty ball cartridges on Friday 25 March 1892.

Chris Sharp of Old Barnsley

children with her. That evening at about 7.00pm, according to the shop assistant who served him, Brocksom went to Messrs Reynolds and Wadsworth, ironmongers, at 18 Church Street. There he purchased from Albert Bright a six-chambered revolver and a box of fifty ball cartridges. Mr Bright told Brocksom that he could try the revolver if he liked and he loaded one of the chambers for him. Brocksom went to the back of the premises and fired the gun at some steps. Brocksom then asked Mr Bright if he would load the gun for him. Mr Bright filled all six chambers then wrapped the revolver up and handed it to Brocksom.

At 4.30am the following morning, Saturday 26 March, the Brocksoms were in bed. Martha Brocksom woke her husband and told him it was time to go to work. He told her he wasn't going to work that day and so they both went back to sleep. Martha Brocksom got up at nine o'clock. Her husband stayed in bed until noon. After eating his breakfast he sat in front of the fire, in his shirt sleeves, without a waistcoat. Martha Brocksom sat on a low stool by the fender, at the edge of the fireplace, sewing. At about a quarter to two Frederick Brocksom asked his wife if she meant what she had said to him the previous day. He repeated the question several times and his wife reiterated that she had indeed meant it, that if he fell out of work she would leave him and take the children and all her belongings with her. Frederick Brocksom was sitting with his hands in his pockets. Martha Brocksom was sitting with her head lowered, concentrating on her sewing. Suddenly out of the corner of her eye she saw her husband lunge at her and she heard a loud report and felt something pass by quickly close to her head. She jumped up and ran out of the house. As she did so she heard another loud report. She went immediately to the house next door, No. 29, and saw her neighbour, Mrs Chappell. Within a few minutes Mr Abraham Chappell arrived home. Just as Martha Brocksom was telling him what had happened two shots were heard coming from her house. Accompanied by Mr Chappell, Martha Brocksom went back home. Her brother, thirteen-year-old George Hanson, who lived with the Brocksoms, had arrived home from work in the short time she was out. As George Hanson went into the house he saw his brother-in-law sitting on a chair in the kitchen in front of a mirror, which was on the wringing machine. Frederick Brocksom's throat was cut and bleeding and there was a carving knife lying on the board beside the mirror.

Brocksom said to his brother-in-law: 'See George, I have been trying to frighten our Martha with this,' at the same time pointing to a revolver which was on the set-pot close to where Martha Brocksom had been sitting. George snatched the revolver but Brocksom took it from him and placed it once again on the set-pot but George snatched it back and ran out of the house, returning a few moments later with Mr Chappell. When they went into the house Brocksom was standing in front of the mirror with the carving knife in his hand. Mr Chappell took the knife from him and returned to his own house with it, then he sent for the police before returning to the Brocksom's house. Frederick Brocksom also told Mr Chappell that he had been trying to frighten Martha, this time adding that he had been firing blank cartridges and had fired two into the ceiling to make her believe he had shot himself and to make her come back to the house. When Mr Chappell asked him what he had done it for, Brocksom replied: 'I cannot live without her. She has deceived me, and I want to die.'

PC Raven arrived at the house at 2.20pm and was shortly followed by Dr Frederick S Barber, house surgeon at the Beckett Hospital. When Constable Raven asked Brocksom what he had been doing, Brocksom said that he had been cutting his throat,

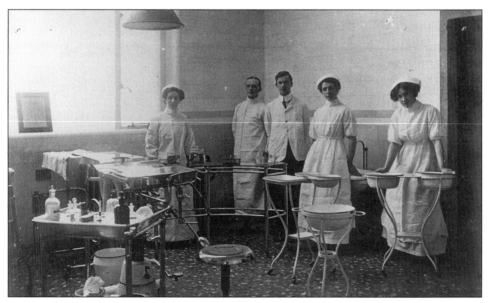

Beckett Hospital, Barnsley, where Frederick Brocksom was taken to receive treatment for self-inflicted injuries to his throat. Chris Sharp of Old Barnsley

then added: 'It's a pity the knife wasn't sharp or it would have done it.' Dr Barber examined Brocksom's wound. It was an inch and three quarters in length and was deep enough to have opened the windpipe. Dr Barber dressed the wound before ordering Brocksom's removal to Beckett Hospital. He accompanied Brocksom to the hospital with PC Raven.

At Barnsley Court House Mr John Carrington cross-examined Martha Brocksom regarding her version of events.

Mr Carrington: *Have you lived happily with the prisoner?*

Martha Brocksom: *No, I have not.*

Mr Carrington: *I gather from that there have been numerous quarrels between you?*

Martha Brocksom: *Yes, there have.*

Mr Carrington: *If you will kindly take your mind back to Friday, the 25th March, as I understand you had a quarrel that day?*

Martha Brocksom: *Yes.*

Mr Carrington: *And, as you've told my friend Mr Catterell, you said to him then that you should leave him if he became out of work?*

Martha Brocksom: *Yes.*

Mr Carrington: *You had often told him that before, hadn't you?*

Martha Brocksom: *Yes, several times.*

Mr Carrington: *You have requested him many a time to leave you, haven't you?*

Martha Brocksom: *Yes.*

Mr Carrington: *Has he told you when you have made those requests, that he should not; that he could not live without you?*

Martha Brocksom: *Yes.*

Mr Carrington: *That has been his invariable reply?*

Martha Brocksom: *Yes.*

Mr Carrington: *Still keeping to the Friday, he had been to work that morning, hadn't he?*

Martha Brocksom: *Yes.*

Mr Carrington: *Did he tell you that he had heard certain reports about you at the bakehouse?*

Martha Brocksom: *Yes.*

Mr Carrington: *And did he, in the course of the quarrel which took place upon that, charge you with being unfaithful to him?*

Martha Brocksom: *Yes.*

Mr Carrington: *What did you say to that?*

Martha Brocksom: *I told him that if he liked to believe it, he could do.*

Mr Carrington: *And I believe later on that day you denied that you had been unfaithful to him?*

Martha Brocksom: *Yes.*

Mr Carrington: *What time did he return home on Friday evening?*

Martha Brocksom: *About nine o'clock.*

Mr Carrington: *Did he go out again that night?*

Martha Brocksom: *No.*

Mr Carrington: *Were you on speaking terms and friendly during the night?*

Martha Brocksom: *I asked him if he wanted some supper; that was all that passed.*

Mr Carrington: *On the Saturday morning had you any conversation at all with him?*

Martha Brocksom: *Yes.*

Mr Carrington: *After he got up at twelve o'clock?*

Martha Brocksom: *Yes.*

Mr Carrington: *Was the conversation of a quarrelsome nature?*

Martha Brocksom: *Yes; it was as to what had been said on the Friday.*

Mr Carrington: *Relative to what I have referred to?*

Martha Brockson: *Yes.*

Mr Carrington: *And in the course of that you struck him?*

Martha Brocksom: *Yes, well the little boy came in, and...*

Mr Carrington: *Never mind the little boy; did you strike him with a brush on the head?*

Martha Brocksom: *Yes.*

The Clerk: *Was it a sweeping brush?*

Martha Brocksom: *Yes.*

The Clerk: *A long one?*

Martha Brocksom: *Yes*

Mr Carrington: *After that he was sitting down for some time before the fire, wasn't he?*

Martha Brocksom: *Yes.*

Mr Carrington: *On which side, right or left?*

Martha Brocksom: *In front of the fire, in the centre.*

Mr Carrington: *And you have described him as sitting with both hands in his pockets?*

Martha Brocksom: *Yes.*

Mr Carrington: *Had you the slightest suspicion that he had anything in either of those pockets then?*

Martha Brocksom: *No, not the slightest.*

Mr Carrington: *Nor had he done anything up to that time to lead you to suppose he was going to injure you, or try to?*

Martha Brocksom: *No.*

Mr Carrington: *What distance apart from you was your husband sitting?*

Martha Brocksom: *Not far.*

Mr Carrington: *By extending his arm he could have touched you?*

Martha Brocksom: *Yes.*

Mr Carrington: *In your examination in chief you said he made a rush at you. If he was as near as you tell me he was, what do you mean by that?*

Martha Brocksom: *I don't know; I didn't see what he did.*

Mr Carrington: *Well, but you said that?*

Martha Brocksom: *I saw him coming to me.*

Mr Carrington: *Well, what rush did he make? Did he simply get up from his chair, and is that the rush you refer to? I should think so.*

The Chairman (John Dyson): *What do you mean by rushing? Were you sitting at the time?*

Martha Brocksom: *Yes.*

Mr Carrington: *And attending to your work, not to your husband?*

Martha Brocksom: *Yes.*

The Chairman: *And when you saw him get up from his chair and move towards you, what did you do?*

Martha Brocksom: *I got up.*

The Chairman: *You got up?*

Martha Brocksom: *Yes; I moved my head first.*

The Clerk: *She said she bent her head forward sir.*

The Chairman: *What made you move your head? Were you apprehensive that he would strike you, or something?*

Martha Brocksom: *Yes, I thought he was going to hit me, and I moved my head, and then I heard a shot.*

The Chairman: *When he seemed in a hurry to get to you, did he get up from his chair?*

Martha Brocksom: *Yes.*

The Chairman: *And moved towards you?*

The Clerk: *Got up from his chair and seemed in a hurry, to what?*

Martha Brocksom: *To get to me.*

Mr Carrington: *And was it then immediately that you heard the shot?*

Martha Brocksom: *Yes.*

Mr Carrington: *And you rushed out of the house?*

Martha Brocksom: *Yes.*

Mr Carrington: *Previous to this Saturday, when you have had* *these quarrels that I have had to refer to, has your husband been subject to fits of depression afterwards?*

Martha Brocksom: *Yes.*

Mr Carrington*: And is it your opinion that he always has been, and is even now, very fond of you?*

Martha Brocksom: *Yes.*

Mr Carrington: *There was no one to prevent his shooting you on the Saturday morning if he had liked, was there?*

Martha Brocksom: *No.*

Mr Carrington: *You have heard the explanation given to your brother by your husband, that he was trying to frighten you?*

Martha Brocksom: *Yes.*

Mr Carrington: *Do you think that was his intention or not?*

Martha Brocksom: *I don't know.*

The Chairman: *You say in your evidence that you have repeatedly said you would leave your husband?*

Martha Brocksom: *Yes.*

The Chairman: *Before this quarrel?*

Martha Brocksom: *Oh, yes.*

The Chairman: *Was that when he was out of work, or was it when he was in work, or both?*

Martha Brocksom: *Oh, no; when he was in work.*

The Chairman: *You have said you would leave him when he was in work?*

Martha Brocksom: *Yes.*

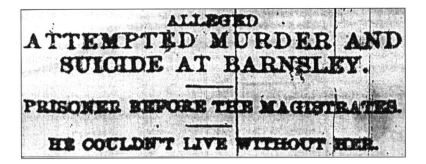

ALLEGED
ATTEMPTED MURDER AND SUICIDE AT BARNSLEY.

PRISONER BEFORE THE MAGISTRATES.

HE COULDN'T LIVE WITHOUT HER.

Having heard the evidence the magistrates committed Frederick William Brocksom to be tried at the next assizes.

Brocksom was tried at Leeds Assizes on Thursday 26 May 1892 before Mr Justice Charles. He was charged with shooting with intent to murder, of firing with intent to do grievous bodily harm and with attempting to commit suicide. Mr James Beverley prosecuted. After hearing the evidence for the prosecution Brocksom made a long rambling statement on his own behalf. In his address to the jury, Brocksom said when he went to live at Barnsley his wife got among relatives and friends and commenced drinking in public houses. He said that he objected to this and also to the fact that she would allow gentlemen to pay for drinks for her. She also went to theatres and music halls, and ultimately this came to the knowledge of his employers, as a result of which he had to leave his work. He also alleged that his wife had told him the sooner he went away the better, as she had got someone else. The fact that there had been a recent shooting case in Barnsley had caused him to think that he would buy a revolver and frighten her. Brockson them rambled on about his health having broken down in consequence of the stories about his wife's conduct having reached the ears of his employers who had told him he would have to leave if there was no improvement. His spirits had got low and he thought if he committed suicide he would be out of the way. He added that his wife had said she wouldn't care if he committed suicide, only he mustn't do it in the house and make a mess. He said she recommended that he should go and throw himself into 't' cut [canal]'. She wouldn't be sorry and wouldn't grieve about him.

Regarding the shooting and his attempt to frighten her, Brocksom said he had aimed over her head and did not intend to injure her, as he could have done so had he wished. The judge during his lengthy summing up said that the miserable relations which existed between the parties were consistent with the supposition that the prisoner shot at his wife with the intention of killing her or of doing her grievous bodily harm. But the evidence in support of it was of the slightest possible character, and it was very doubtful to him whether the prisoner shot at the woman at all or whether, if he did, he intended to injure her at all. The judge also pointed out that Brocksom had always treated his wife well, and that she would not be sorry, judging from her appearance in the witness box, to be rid of him. The jury having considered their verdict found Brocksom not guilty of shooting with attempt to murder and also of firing with intent to do grievous bodily harm. On the charge of attempting to commit suicide, Brocksom was found guilty. Mr Justice Charles sentenced Brocksom to three months' imprisonment without hard labour, to take effect from the date of his incarceration the previous month.

CHAPTER 9

A Mother's Murder of Innocents, Kendray, 1942

...there were no other injuries except deep cuts right across the throats.

On the morning of Friday 6 November 1942, thirty-six-year-old ARP ambulance driver Gilbert Foster returned home from night duty to 15 Poplars Road, Kendray, where he found four members of his family covered in blood with wounds to their throats. His two daughters, both dressed in their night clothes, lay side by side in a double bed in the front bedroom. Rosemary aged five and Sylvia just ten months old were dead. Their throats had been slit open. Mr Foster's twelve-year-old son Thomas was in the back bedroom and his thirty-four-year-old wife, Annie, was in the living room. Both Thomas and Annie Foster were still alive and each had wounds to their throats.

Mr Foster called Ada Lee of 14 Poplars Road to the house about 6.40am, then went to fetch a doctor. Mrs Lee had known the Fosters for about five years. When she arrived at No. 15 she saw Mrs Foster sitting in a chair in the living room. Mrs Lee said that Annie Foster's lips were blackened and she could see a gash in her throat. Mrs Foster said: 'I have taken some poison – permanganate of potash,' and a few moments later uttered the words: 'My poor bairns!' Dr A B Slack arrived and the police were also soon on the scene. Mrs Foster and her son were taken to Beckett Hospital in Barnsley. Fortunately the boy's injuries were not severe and he soon recovered.

Barnsley Tragedy

FATHER FINDS FAMILY WITH THROAT WOUNDS

TWO CHILDREN DEAD

The Chief Constable, Mr H T Williams and several other police officers spent most of the morning at the house and took away a carving knife, which had been found by Sergeant Herring on a chair near the bed where the girls had died. The bodies of the two girls were removed to Barnsley Mortuary where Ernest Foster, firewatcher, of 36a Buckley Street, identified them as his nieces. A post-mortem examination carried out by Professor P L Sutherland, concluded that there were no other injuries except deep cuts right across the throats. The cuts were jagged as if they had been hacked and it appeared that the knife had been drawn across the girls' throats seven or eight times. It was quite obvious that the cause of death in each case were these injuries. The bodies of both children were well developed and well nourished. An inquest held on the bodies of Rosemary and Sylvia Foster was opened by District Coroner Mr C J Haworth on Monday 9 November and adjourned until 8 December.

During her stay in hospital Annie Foster made a statement to the police Sergeant Lickiss:

There is something I'd like to say, but I'm afraid it may cause bother for my husband. That is what made me do this. There

Part of the council estate in Kendray where the Foster family lived in 1942. Chris Sharp of Old Barnsley

was a man came to my house to start collecting. I thought he
was a man who had seen me, when I went a ride in a car with
a certain fellow. He did not do me no wrong in one way, but I
think it was that that upset my nerve. That is what I thought.
You see this fellow coming sort of unbalanced me I suppose.
Did I ought to say his name? Well I was thinking it might seem
something very serious for my husband, with me having done
this. I have not been a bad girl. That is all I have to say.

Annie Foster was discharged from hospital on 19 November when she was charged with the murder of her daughter, Rosemary. On being charged she replied: 'Is there just one of them?' In answer to the charge of murdering Sylvia she asked: 'Is that the same day?' and on the charge of feloniously wounding her son Thomas, she said: 'No. I did not intend to do that. I did not intend that with any of them.' On the charge of attempting to commit suicide, she replied: 'I am not saying anything, because I don't follow dates.'

On Thursday 7 January 1943, thirty-four-year-old Annie Foster appeared before magistrates at Barnsley County Borough Police Court, charged with the wilful murder of her children Rosemary and Sylvia and with feloniously wounding her son; and with attempting to commit suicide on or about 6 November 1942. The chairman of the bench was Alderman Joseph Jones CBE LLD, with whom sat Miss England and Councillor H M Cassels. Mrs Foster pleaded not guilty and reserved her defence. She was represented by Mr L Wagstaffe.

During the course of the hearing it transpired that for some time Mrs Foster had harboured the fear that the country was about to be invaded and that the Germans were coming. She had told her husband if they did come they would cut the throats of their children and her own. Her conviction that this was the case was further cemented when Germany invaded Russia and she expressed the view that England would be invaded any day soon. She had become obsessed with some insurance policies she had taken out on her husband and her parents. Gilbert Foster commented that these policies for no apparent reason had been a source of his wife's great depression and anxiety.

Mr D J Osborne, prosecuting on behalf of the Director of Public Prosecutions told the court that on 5 November Mr Foster left to go on duty at about 5.45pm. He returned briefly to the house at about 9.00pm with some chips that he had

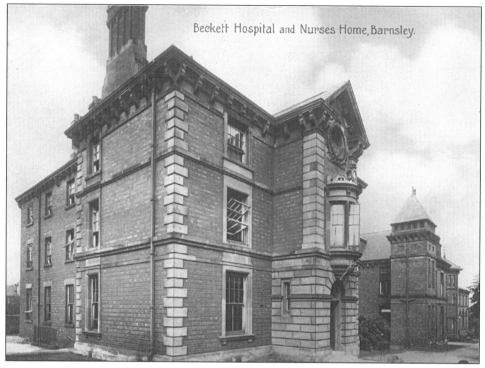

Beckett Hospital, Barnsley, where Mrs Annie Foster and her son Thomas were taken at about 7am on Friday 6 November 1942. Author's collection

promised to get for the family. He found the house locked and had difficulty gaining admission. Mrs Foster eventually opened the door and she asked her husband: 'Is there anyone else with you?' When he replied 'No', their son, Tommy said: 'She was frightened a man was coming.' Mr Foster went back to his depot and returned home again to check all was well at about eleven o'clock when he found the door was locked. When Mrs Foster admitted him she was accompanied by their son who despite the late hour was fully dressed. Mr Foster remonstrated with Tommy that he ought to be in bed, he replied: 'I am in bed. All in the same bed.' Mrs Foster had taken all three children to bed with her and young Tommy had been laying fully clothed across the bottom of the bed. Mr Foster told Tommy to get undressed and he, having done so, his father took him to his proper bedroom. Before Mr Foster left for the depot again his wife appeared to be a little more cheerful and on parting Mr Foster told her not to worry about the insurance policies as her father would be coming the following morning to tell her that everything was all right.

At 6.10am the following morning Mr Foster returned home and made a gruesome discovery. On opening the door he heard his wife getting up. As he went into the kitchen he heard his wife coming downstairs. He went to the living room and was dumfounded to see his wife holding an eiderdown to her throat which was bleeding profusely. Mr Foster rushed upstairs and pulled back the bedclothes of their double bed. His two daughters lay dead, besmeared in blood. He dashed to Tommy's room and found him injured but still alive. Mr Foster hurriedly left the house, fetched a neighbour, Mrs Ada Lee, then went immediately to Dr Slack's house, before going to the ambulance station and returning home with an ambulance. Dr Slack had meanwhile telephoned the police and gone to Poplars Road. Tommy was conscious and the bleeding had stopped. Dr Slack dressed Tommy's wounds. He concluded that the girls had died about three hours earlier at around 3.30am. On coming downstairs Mrs Foster told him that she had taken poison and the Germans were coming.

Mr Osborne said that investigations had been made into the accused's statement and these had shown that they had no foundation in fact. It was quite true that she went to a hospital in a man's car but this was at her husband's request. That was all that had happened. Mr Osborne also said that about a month before the tragedy the Civil Defence authority had sent a letter to Mr Foster regarding steps to be taken in the event of an invasion. This letter had been open by Mrs Foster and its contents had clearly added to her concerns.

Married in 1929, the marriage on the whole had been a happy one but from time to time Mrs Foster was very bad tempered and suffered from periodic bouts of extreme rage. During these periods she appeared to be an entirely different woman but afterwards returned to her normal condition. The arrival of a new baby ten months before the murders occurred had added to Mrs Foster's problems and she had received medical attention for headaches. Mr Osborne asked that the accused should be committed for trial at Leeds Assizes.

Annie Foster by then aged thirty-five, was tried at Leeds Assizes on Monday 15 March 1943 before Mr Justice Cassels. Mr Myles Archibald prosecuted. Defending counsel was Mr J McLusky, instructed by Messrs Halmshaw and Wagstaffe of Barnsley. Dr G A McCormick, the medical officer of

Manchester Prison was called as a defence witness. He testified that in his opinion at the time of the tragedy the accused was suffering from acute mental breakdown. She would know the nature and quality of her actions but would not be capable of forming a rational judgement as to know that her acts were wrong. In her evidence Mrs Foster said that she went up to bed at about 9.00pm. She had a knife with her but she did not know why she had taken it to bed. She woke about three o'clock and got out of bed. She said that she felt dizzy and could not remember the events that followed. When her husband returned from work the following morning she thought the Germans had come with him.

The jury retired to consider their verdict and returned after a short interval with a verdict of 'guilty but insane when the act was committed.' The judge ordered that Annie Foster should be detained until His Majesty's pleasure be known.

CHAPTER 10

Women's Land Army Girl Murdered by Glassworks Engineer, Barnsley, 1943

Her mother told me I was jealous of Bob but if she had known as much as me she would have murdered her...

On Saturday 8 May 1943 the *Barnsley Chronicle* reported:

About 8.50 a.m. on Tuesday [4 May] *a Land Army girl was found inside the 'Dodgem' machines corrugated iron enclosure on Barnsley Fairground between the* Wellington Hotel *and the* Wire Trellis Hotel *suffering from severe head injuries. She lay huddled on the ground just inside the darkened entrance.*

Barnsley Fairground seen here during the Whitsuntide Fair in 1937.

Chris Sharp of Old Barnsley

*The entrances are so designed that though there is no infringe-
ment of the black-out regulations they are always open.*

Mrs Anne Tuby, proprietress of the fair made the discovery. The
emergency services were immediately summoned. As the
injured girl, who was wearing a Women's Land Army uniform,
was removed to the ambulance a bloodstained hammer was
found under her body. She was taken to Barnsley Beckett
Hospital. At first it was thought the girl had been laying there all
night but a bus ticket in her possession showed she had travelled
to Barnsley early that morning.

Chief Constable H T Williams, Detective Inspector R S
Harrison and several other police officers were quickly at the
crime scene and within a few hours the girl's identity was
established as Miss Violet Wakefield, a Women's Land Army girl,
aged twenty, of 27 The Grove, Cudworth. Her father Thomas
Wakefield, a miner at Grimethorpe Colliery had already left for

*The Beckett Hospital where the severely injured Women's Land Army Girl, Violet
Wakefield was taken on the morning of Tuesday 4 May 1943.* Author's collection

South Yorkshire Times

work early in the afternoon. Following the injured girl's discovery, after police called at the family home, Mr Wakefield was brought back from work and accompanied by his wife went to Barnsley Beckett Hospital. There they sat at their daughter's bedside. Violet did not regain consciousness and died at 3.50pm that same afternoon. Scotland Yard detectives were called in to assist Barnsley police. Chief Inspector Beveridge and Detective Sergeant Webb of New Scotland Yard arrived in Barnsley early on Tuesday evening. At 8.30pm, accompanied by Inspector Harrison, they saw Violet Wakefield's body in the mortuary at Barnsley Beckett Hospital.

Twenty-year-old Violet Wakefield had joined the Women's Land Army in February 1943. She had first been detailed to work with Bill Oakes, a lorry driver, whom she had assisted to load and unload agricultural machinery. Each morning she travelled to a farm in Cawthorne from her Cudworth home, a journey that took her on two buses. The first from Cudworth to Barnsley, leaving Cudworth at 7.25am, then another from Barnsley Bus Station to Cawthorne Basin, which left Barnsley at 8.00am. She drove a tractor on a farm and Violet was said to be very fond of her work. She had previously worked at a Barnsley glassworks, Wood Brothers Glass Company Limited. While working at the glassworks Violet had met Trevor Elvin, a tall well-built, good-looking youth, and they had begun a relationship which had lasted for about two years. It emerged that on the morning Violet Wakefield was attacked Trevor Elvin left the house where he lived with his parents, 24 Grove Street, Barnsley. Witnesses reported having seen him meeting Violet at the bus stop near the top of Pontefract Road at 7.45am. They were last seen together walking near the *Wire Trellis Hotel* and by the fairground. Between 8.50am and 8.55.am Elvin was seen hurrying back down Pontefract Road and, according to his mother, arrived home at about 8.00am. Elvin's father was away serving in the forces. Shortly after he had arrived home Elvin left the house and told his aunt, Mrs Cooper, he would be back in a minute. A little after 11.00am Elvin called on his uncle at Otley. He told his uncle, Arthur Lyons, a butcher, that he had got a lift with a pal from Barnsley and was going to Leeds. He said he wanted to buy his girl, Vi, a present, a gold disk costing 18s. 6d. but had come without money. His uncle lent him £1. Elvin was next seen in Blackpool, at about 6.30pm, standing outside the premises of another uncle, Ernest Lyons, a caterer. When his uncle asked him what he was doing

Elvin replied:

I don't know. I don't remember.

His uncle was somewhat perturbed by this odd reply and took Elvin to Blackpool Police Station, where Elvin told PC Walmsley:

I have had a row with my girl.

PC Walmsley advised Mr Lyons to get his nephew a night's lodgings. Later that evening PC Walmsley read a newspaper report, which resulted in him phoning Barnsley Police Station and speaking to Chief Inspector Beveridge of New Scotland Yard. The telephone call resulted in PC Walmsley and others going to Elvin's lodgings and asking him to accompany them back to Blackpool Police Station. In his possession were two letters, three photographs and a diary.

One letter written to Violet's parents read:

Dear Mr. and Mrs. Wakefield,

You may think I am a rotter taking your Vi away from you. It is for the best. She used to tell me Bob was bow-legged, bald and about 40 years old, but during a bit of talking we settled things up a bit. First of all she told me what had happened between her and Bob. Then I told her one or two things I knew she had owned up to and they were one of the lowest tricks you can find in the town. Why was she finishing at 5.30 and not getting home while 8.30? You did not know nothing but I got to know something which I could not stand.

The other letter read:

Dear Mum and Dad,

Don't think that I am lowering your good name by doing this to Vi. She is the only one in the world to look to. I have done everything in my power to let her have what she wanted but she told me this holiday what had been going off with her and Bob. Her mother told me I was jealous of Bob but if she had known as much as me she would have murdered her. Well, give my love to all I know. Goodbye. Mum and Dad, not forgetting my Granma, which I know it will be a shock to her. But Granma can't you see she has done the dirty on me, one

of the lowest ways in the world.
> *With all my love.*
> *Trev (One of the silly boys out of thousands)*

On the back of one photograph Elvin had written:

Dear Jack,
> *I am sorry I have had to do this, but it's the only way out.*
> *I have never done wrong while I have been going with Violet,*
> *bless her but after what she told me I had to do it. She has told*
> *nothing but lies since she has been with Bob.*

On the back of a photograph of Violet Wakefield and addressed to the dead girl, he had written:

Dear Vi,
> *You told me everything tonight about you and Bob. I*
> *can't believe it is true. Goodbye, goodbye, darling Hope to be*
> *with you soon.*

At the bottom of the photograph was written:

Dear Violet,
> *Please accept ring and photo from me, as I will not need*
> *them in future. Well, I only hope you find someone in your way*
> *as good as I have been. Remember me to all at 27. – Trev*

The diary contained the following entry:

I am sure Violet is in love with Bob but he will never win her.
I am not jealous of Violet but she has changed from good to
worse.

Following an early morning drive to Blackpool by detectives, Elvin was collected from the police station there and brought back to Barnsley. On his way back to Barnsley in the police car Elvin fell asleep. When he woke he said:

My head is clearer now and things are coming back to me. I
saw Vi yesterday morning at the bus and we walked together
as far as the Wire Trellis. I can't remember anything more until
I found myself on the front at Blackpool.

At 6.45am in company with New Scotland Yard Officers Detective Chief Inspector Beveridge and Detective Sergeant Webb, Detective Inspector Harrison of Barnsley Police visited twenty-one-year-old Trevor Elvin in his cell at Barnsley Borough Police Station and told him they were making enquiries into the death of Violet Wakefield and were going to charge him with murder, to which Elvin made no reply. He later made a statement in which he said:

Vi has been in the Land Army for four months and since then there have been one or two little tiffs between us, but we have always made it up. About Christmas time last year Vi and I discussed getting married but I saw that I could not afford it and we talked of getting married at Whitsun – that was at this coming Whitsun. We started to save up together. I had given her £5 and she had put £2 10s. to it. I gave her the money before Easter and she kept asking for a dress ring. I told her I would give her an engagement ring and it was agreed that we should get engaged at Easter Saturday. When I saw Vi on Good Friday she was still keen on getting engaged on the following day, and we had arranged to buy the ring, but when I met her on Easter Saturday she said she had no more feeling to get married and did not want to get engaged. We had a few words about this but nothing serious, and I told her that if she did not want to be engaged I could not make her. We continued to see each other and on Easter Sunday I asked her if she had any other fellow on her mind. She told me she had none, but I thought there was as she was too friendly with a man, Bob, who worked on a lorry with her. On many occasions I would go to her house about half-past six in the evening to see Vi as that was her usual time for getting home, but often I waited until half-past eight or nine o'clock. I spoke to her about this and asked her where she had been, and she told me she had been talking to Bob. This upset me very much and we had several tiffs about it. The last of these tiffs was on Monday evening last. Vi promised to meet me at the bus station at ten minutes to six. I went there but she did not turn up. I was walking home when I met my mother. We met Vi at the bottom of Grove Street, coming from our house. We left my mother and I went with Vi to her home. We were quarrelling practically all the time. At first she said she had been to the bus station to meet me, but I told her I thought she was lying and that she had come on Bob's lorry to Oakwell Lane. I left Val at her house at half-past nine that evening and promised to meet her at 7.50 a.m. the next day at the top of Pontefract Road to give her some cigarettes. I went straight home feeling depressed and down. Everyone was in bed and I sat down and wrote notes to Mr. And Mrs. Wakefield, my Mum and Dad, my brother Jack, my sister Gladys, and one to Vi. All these notes were found on me by the police at Blackpool. When I wrote these notes it was my intention to clear out of it and forget all about Vi. After writing these notes I went to bed but could not sleep and kept thinking things over. When I got up next morning I made up my mind to frighten Vi when I saw her and before I went out I put a hammer in my raincoat pocket. I got the hammer from the top of the cellar steps. It had a broken end. I met Vi as arranged and she asked me for the cigarettes. I told her I had none and she said: "I will get somebody else to buy me some." I asked her who the somebody else was but she did not reply. We walked together to the Gas Nook. When we got to the Wire Trellis, which is opposite to the fairground, I showed her the hammer. I don't remember anything after this until I was on a bus. I got off this bus at Dewsbury and then went to Leeds and later to Otley, where I saw my uncle, Arthur Lyons. I borrowed £1 from him, telling him I was going to Leeds. I went back to Leeds and after walking round I went to Manchester by train. The next I remember was finding myself on the front at Blackpool…

On Thursday 6 May glassworks engineer Trevor Elvin stood in the dock between two policemen before the Barnsley County Borough magistrates charged with the murder of Violet Wakefield. He never spoke throughout the proceedings. Detective Inspector Harrison asked for a remand in custody until Thursday 27 May. On being asked if he had any objection to being remanded Elvin shook his head and on being asked if he had any solicitor appearing for him he again shook his head. Mr P St John-Carrington, the magistrates' clerk pointed out to Elvin that he was entitled to have assigned to him legal aid and asked if he would like to have assigned to him any solicitor acting in this court. To this question Elvin nodded his head. The remand in custody was granted and Elvin was granted a legal aid certificate which assigned both a solicitor and counsel to him.

On Friday 7 May an inquest was opened and adjourned at Barnsley Town Hall by Deputy Coroner Mr S H B Gill on the body of Violet Wakefield. At the inquest Mrs Annie Tuby, then living in a caravan on the temporary fairground said at 8.50am on Tuesday 4 May she walked through the dodgems, which are enclosed on the fairground and belonged to her sons. She saw what at first she thought were some potato sacks inside near the entrance. At about twelve feet away she got the impression it was a man asleep on the floor. She became frightened, walked outside and shouted to three men working nearby. She said she did not realize it was a Land Army girl. She added that if there had been any screaming she would have heard it from her caravan. Police War Reserve Albert Turton said on the morning of Tuesday 4 May he was on point duty at the bottom of New Street. At 8.55am, in consequence of something that was said to him he went to the dodgem ride situated near the *Wellington Hotel.* In the entrance to the right he saw a young woman dressed in Land Army uniform. She was lying face downwards on the ground with her feet towards the entrance. When the coroner asked if she was fully dressed PC Turton said that she was, excepting the hat which lay a short distance away (the hat's cord had been torn away at one side and in the bloodstained crown were several holes). He added that the girl had severe head injuries and was bleeding profusely. She was unconscious and on finding she was still alive PC Turton said he summoned assistance and an ambulance was sent for. Shortly before the girl was taken to hospital PC Turton said he found a hammer, partly beneath her, which appeared to be bloodstained.

West Riding County Council Pathologist, Professor P L Sutherland who conducted the post-mortem examination on Miss Wakefield's body said she was a well nourished, well developed girl, 5ft 1in in height, with no sign of any disease. There were seventeen lacerated wounds on the scalp from ¾ inch to 2½ inches in length, fractures of the vault of the skull and severe injuries to the brain. There was an abrasion of the palm of the hand. The injury to the hand was consistent with her putting her hand up to protect herself. Professor Sutherland said abrasions on the knees were consistent with falling in the struggle. Death was caused by extensive fractures of the vault of the skull and severe injuries to the brain; and haemorrhage. These injuries were caused by a heavy blunt instrument with a narrow striking surface. A hammer found beneath the victim's unconscious body was produced and Professor Sutherland said it could have caused such injuries. He said that he counted seventeen blows to the head and some of the larger wounds were caused by more than one blow striking one part. War Reserve Police Constable Albert Turton identified the hammer as the one found under the body.

Thomas Wakefield said his daughter had been keeping company with Trevor Elvin for about two years. When asked by the coroner if the couple were engaged, Mr Wakefield replied: 'No.' When asked if it was his daughter's custom to meet Elvin on her way to work, Mr Wakefield said that it was not but she sometimes said Elvin would wave to her as her bus passed Wood's glassworks. When asked if they got on well together Mr Wakefield said that they did for a time but later they had little tiffs, nothing serious.

The coroner said that he had received notification that a charge of wilful murder had been made against Trevor Elvin. Therefore at this point he proposed to adjourn the inquest pending the termination of the criminal proceedings. He added that the jury might not be called together again and he therefore proposed they make a finding as to the cause of death. He asked if they agreed to the cause of death as stated by Professor Sutherland. The jury agreed and it was so recorded.

On 15 May the *Barnsley Chronicle* reported:

Wide public sympathy was demonstrated at the funeral of Miss Violet Wakefield on Saturday [8 May]. *All along the route from the house to Cudworth Parish Church blinds were drawn and silent crowds watched the passing of the cortege. The Vicar (Rev. G. H. Stanney) conducted the service inside the church preceding internment in the churchyard. Private mourners were Mr. And Mrs. Thomas Wakefield (father and mother), Harry, Thomas and Ronald (brothers),, the mother's relatives from Deal, Kent, and a large number of other relatives and friends. There was a strong following of members of the Women's Land Army, and employees (glasshouse girls predominating) of Wood Bros. Glass Co. Ltd. , where Miss Wakefield was employed previous to joining the Land Army. Among a striking display of floral tokens were wreaths from most of the Land Army depots in Yorkshire.*

At Barnsley Borough Police Court on Tuesday 7 June Trevor Elvin appeared before magistrates Alderman J Jones (chairman), Mrs Allum and Councillor J Richards, charged with the wilful murder of Violet Wakefield. Elvin pleaded not guilty.

Mr J F Caxton prosecuted on behalf of the Director of Public Prosecutions and Mr Myles Archibald, instructed by Mr L Wagstaffe of Barnsley, appeared for Elvin. Witness information largely reiterated that previously heard at the inquest.

PC Walmsley of Blackpool Police said when Trevor Elvin's Uncle, Mr Ernest Lyons saw him at Blackpool Police Station he said to him:

> *This is my sister's son who arrived from Barnsley this morning. He is very strange in his manner and I am at a loss what to do with him.*

Mr Lyons said that the accused could not tell him why he had come to Blackpool or how. He was crying but to all questions he simply answered, 'I don't know.' Lyons said he took the accused to a hotel where they had drinks. In another hotel he bought Elvin three pints of beer thinking that this might induce him to open up and tell him what was troubling him, but to all questions he again answered, 'I don't know.'

Robert Oakes of 168 Higham Common Road, Barugh Green, lorry driver, employed by the War Agricultural Committee said that Miss Wakefield finished work at 5.30pm on 3 May and as they were returning from Pontefract to Cawthorne he dropped her in Barnsley. Mr Archibald made an application for special medical advice in view of the nature of the defence he proposed to put forward. The certificate was granted. At the conclusion of the proceedings Elvin was committed for trial at the next Leeds Sessions.

Trevor Elvin's trial began at Leeds Assizes on Monday 12 July 1943 before Mr Justice Tucker. Mr Russell Vick, KC and Mr R Cleworth prosecuted. The defence was conducted by Mr G H B Streatfield, KC and Mr Myles Archibald. The trial lasted one day. The evidence was clear and concise, there being little doubt about the sequence of events.

The pathologist, Professor P L Sutherland when asked by Mr Streatfield,

> *Would it be right to assume that the person who inflicted these blows must have done so in an appalling frenzy?* Professor Sutherland replied: *It was certainly an appalling outburst of violence.*

Defence witness Professor W MacAdam of Leeds University

said the evidence and the increasing recollection of Elvin were in keeping with a picture of a quite well recognised type of mental disorder. Mr Streatfield asked Professor MacAdam:

Assuming this was correct and that the accused suffered a blackout. In what mental state would he be?

Professor McAdam replied:

He would be in a state in which he did not know what he was doing.

Lorry driver Robert Oakes was asked by Mr Vick if he had ever met Elvin. Mr Oakes replied:

Yes, on several occasions.

Mr Vick then asked: 'Has he at any time spoken to you about your behaviour towards Violet Wakefield?' to which Mr Oakes replied:

He never spoke to me at all.

When asked by Mr Vick: 'Have you ever conducted yourself to give cause for jealousy?' Mr Oates replied:

No.

Towards the end of the trial Trevor Elvin's mother said her son was one of the best and had never given way to outburst of temper or violence. During the last six months he had been suffering from headaches which had been getting worse. Witness for the prosecution Dr F H Brisby, medical officer at Armley Gaol, Leeds said he formed the opinion that the prisoner was very highly strung and a type of man who would not stand up to stress very well. Dr Brisby attributed Elvin's inability to recollect the events of the morning of 4 May to a repression of a very painful episode. In his address to the jury Mr Streatfield, in speaking for the defence, invited them to return a verdict of 'guilty but insane'. After a retirement of fifty-minutes the jury returned with a guilty verdict and made no other recommendation. Having donned the black cap Mr Justice Tucker pronounced sentence of death. As the death

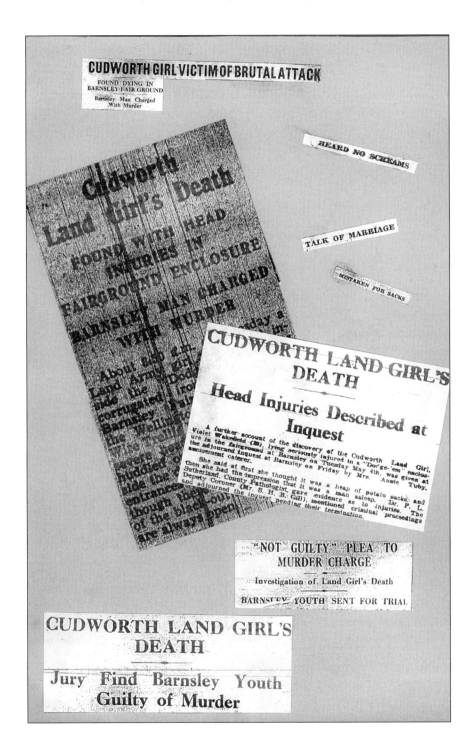

CUDWORTH GIRL VICTIM OF BRUTAL ATTACK

FOUND DYING IN
BARNSLEY FAIR GROUND

Barnsley Man Charged
With Murder

HEARD NO SCREAMS

TALK OF MARRIAGE

MISTAKEN FOR SACKS

Cudworth
Land Girl's Death

FOUND WITH HEAD
INJURIES IN
FAIRGROUND ENCLOSURE

BARNSLEY MAN CHARGED
WITH MURDER

CUDWORTH LAND GIRL'S
DEATH

Head Injuries Described at
Inquest

A further account of the discovery of the Cudworth Land Girl,
Violet Wakefield (20), lying seriously injured in a "Dodge-'em" enclosure in the fairground at Barnsley on Tuesday May 4th, was given at
the adjourned inquest at Barnsley on Friday by Mrs. Annie Toby,
amusement caterer.

She said at first she thought it was a heap of potato sacks, and
then she had the impression that it was a man asleep.   Dr. P. L.
Sutherland, County Pathologist, gave evidence as to injuries. The
Deputy Coroner (Mr. S. H. B. Gill), mentioned criminal proceedings
and adjourned the inquest pending their termination.

"NOT GUILTY" PLEA TO
MURDER CHARGE

Investigation of Land Girl's Death

BARNSLEY YOUTH SENT FOR TRIAL

CUDWORTH LAND GIRL'S
DEATH

Jury Find Barnsley Youth
Guilty of Murder

sentence was pronounced Elvin collapsed and had to be supported by warders. 'Mother', he was heard to utter as he was half carried down the stairs to the cells.

On Thursday 9 September a petition for the reprieve of Trevor Elvin containing 28,436 signatures was handed to the Home Secretary, Mr Herbert Morrison. Among those who had signed their names were Mr Frank Collindridge, MP for Barnsley, Alderman J Jones (who presided over the Police Court hearing), the Mayoress of Barnsley, Mrs S Trueman and the Reverend W Stanhope Lovell, former Chaplain to HM Prison, Dartmoor. Trevor Elvin was hanged the next morning at Armley Gaol, Leeds, Friday 10 September 1943 by Thomas Pierrepoint. The assistant executioner was Harry Kirk. Afterwards his body was buried within Armley Gaol's precincts.

CHAPTER 11

The Green Linnet Murder, Wombwell, 1955

Several minutes into the examination Dr Price discovered a bread knife protruding from the body. This knife had caused injuries to the intestines and had cut into the liver.

In the early hours of Sunday 1 May 1955, night watchman Stanley Steer of 5 Gower Street, Wombwell, was on duty at some road works near Aldham Bridge, Wombwell. As he sat by the brazier outside his cabin he was approached by a stocky, blonde haired, young man who came towards him shouting, laughing and waving his arms about. As the young man leant with his back against the cabin door, he said:

I have just killed my mother-in-law, the whore.

The young man's name was Alec Wilkinson, aged twenty-two, who was estranged from his wife of just nine months and was living at 12 Gerald Walk, Kendray. Mr Steer said that Wilkinson told him he had cut his mother-in-law with a bread knife and described how he had done it with sweeping gestures. Wilkinson also told him that his wife had been selling the furniture and he wanted to know where the money had gone. Mr Steer noticed that Wilkinson was bleeding heavily from a cut to his hand. He refused to have it bandaged and at first Wilkinson would not hear of Mr Steer going for the police but eventually agreed. Mr Steer went and telephoned the police and when he returned a short while later Wilkinson was still standing by the brazier. Mr Steer asked him how old he was and Wilkinson told him he was twenty-one. He asked him if he had a mother and when Wilkinson replied, 'Yes' Mr Steer commented: 'It is a pity you did not think of your mother when you did this.' On hearing these words Wilkinson broke down and started crying. He then said: 'Oh God, what will my mother think.' Wilkinson then handed Mr Steer his wallet and wristwatch and asked him to send them to his mother. He gave Mr Steer her address. Mr Steer noticed that the watch had stopped at twelve o'clock and that it was covered in blood. A fire engine passed by and Wilkinson said: 'There's the fire brigade going to Mitchell's [another name for Bradbury Balk Lane]' Then Wilkinson told Mr Steer that he had got two rubber cushions, set fire to them and thrown them on his mother-in-law.

Shortly after this an ambulance passed by and Wilkinson ran into the road to try and stop it. It carried on and Wilkinson went into the cabin. Wilkinson said that his wife had come into the house and so he got hold of her and jumped on her. He said she had tried to get up but he just kept jumping on her. The police soon arrived and Wilkinson was taken away. Mr Steer handed the wallet and watch to a policeman. One of the notes which protruded from the wallet was covered in blood.

Police Constable A L Wardle, stationed at Barnsley was driving the patrol car which picked Wilkinson up at 1.20am near Aldham Bridge on 1 May. Wilkinson told him: 'I have done my mother-in-law in.' PC Wardle noticed blood on his hands and dark stains on his suit. He cautioned Wilkinson and told him he was arresting him on suspicion of having committed a felony, to which Wilkinson replied: 'I have done her in I tell you. Don't you believe me?' On the journey to Wombwell Police Station Wilkinson remained talkative. PC Wardle said his remarks were interspersed with bursts of unnatural laughter. He added that that Wilkinson did not smell of drink and in his opinion was not drunk.

At Wombwell Police Station later that morning Alec Wilkinson was examined by Dr Price, following him being called in to examine the body of Mrs Clara Farrell. Home Office Pathologist Dr David E Price was attached to the North-Eastern Forensic Laboratory at Harrogate. Wilkinson complained of a headache and an injury to his right hand. On examining the hand, Dr Price found it to be swollen and bruised and cut a little. Dr Price said:

He appeared to be tremulous but he knew what he was doing and where he was and for what reason. He was quite co-operative.

Dr Price noticed a smearing of blood on Wilkinson's trousers and dried blood in the folds of his nails. He took a scraping from

BARNSLEY MAN CHARGED WITH MURDERING HIS MOTHER-IN-LAW

A 21-YEARS-OLD Barnsley miner was charged at Barnsley West Riding Magistrates' Court this week with the wilful murder of his mother-in-law, Mrs. Clara Farrell, of Bradbury Balklane, Wombwell, by stabbing her with a knife. The body of the woman was found in the blazing living room of her home; her daughter was also dragged from the burning house in a serious condition.

The inquest on the dead woman was opened at Barnsley on Wednesday and adjourned pending the result of the criminal proceedings.

A powerfully built, blonde haired miner, whistled softly to himself as he was brought into Barnsley West Riding Magistrates Court on Wednesday handcuffed to a Police officer.

Mr. and Mrs. Alec Wilkinson

He was Alec Wilkinson (21), 12, Gerald-walk, Kendray, who was charged with murdering his mother-in-law Clara Farrell, of Bradbury Balk-lane, Wombwell, by stabbing her with a knife.

He had been in custody since Monday.

On that day he made a brief appearance before the Magistrates and heard Supt. John W. Dunn say: "Alec Wilkinson has been charged with the murder of his mother-in-law late on the night of April 30 or early in the morning of May 1 by stabbing her with a knife."

"After he was arrested he made a voluntary statement to the Police which I do not propose to put in at this stage.

"Further inquiries have to be made about injuries received at the same time by his wife, Maureen Wilkinson, who at the present time is in Beckett Hospital in a serious condition.

"On these facts I apply for a remand in custody until Wednesday."

Wilkinson applied for legal aid which was granted and asked that the Barnsley solicitor, Mr. A. S. McKenzie, should defend him.

On Wednesday, Wilkinson made a two minute appearance and was again remanded in custody until Friday.

He listened with apparent unconcern as Chief Insp. B. E. Vaughan asked for a further remand in custody until Friday as Wilkinson's wife was still dangerously ill in Beckett Hospital.

Throughout the proceedings Wilkinson—a stocky figure in a blue suit and light blue open necked shirt—allowed his gaze to wander all round the courtroom. His lips were pursed as if he was whistling softly to himself. He appeared completely unconcerned and unmoved.

It was only when asked if he had anything to say to the Magistrates that he looked at the members of the Bench.

His reply was "No."

The back of the Court was packed with members of the public. Small knots of people were standing in the street outside the courthouse long before the hearing was due to begin.

Barnsley Chronicle

Wilkinson's nails and later the same day took a sample of his blood.

The lead up to these events began during Barnsley Feast on 21 August 1954 when Alec Wilkinson married Maureen Farrell and they began their short married life at a house next door but one to Maureen's parents at 21 Bradberry Balk Lane, Wombwell. Alec worked at Barnsley Main Colliery. Living in such close proximity to his inlaws, Charles and Clara Farrell of No. 17, Alec gained the opinion that his mother-in-law was not of the highest moral character. Her nickname, 'The Green Linnet', as he soon discovered resulted from her flamboyant attire, possibly used to attract potential male customers in her nefarious periods as a prostitute, rather that as one female witness, said she believed it came about from the name of a greyhound Clara Farrell often placed bets on. He discovered Mrs Farrell was aggressive, domineering and brawling. Soon after the marriage Clara Farrell revealed her true colours when Alec took a day off work because he was not feeling well. A tirade of verbal abuse poured from her lips as she accused him of 'laiking' while Maureen was working. What appears to have been a particularly galling comment made by Clara Farrell to her son-in-law was when she had told him he should go in the army, to which he had replied:

What would happen to Maureen if I did?

She had then intimated that if they were short of money then Maureen should 'go on the game', as she herself had done.

Charles and Clara Farrell were married in 1926. As well as their twenty-one-year-old daughter, Maureen, they also had a son, Charles, aged twenty-four who was serving in the RAF and stationed in Germany. Following her husband's comments that he thought his wife was spending too much time there, Mrs Farrell visited No. 21 less frequently. In January 1955 Alec Wilkinson left his wife and went to live with his parents at 12 Gerald Walk, Kendray. Maureen soon joined her husband there but on February 20 she left Alec and returned to her parents' home, where she remained in residence until the night her mother was killed and she herself was brutally attacked. On 30 April Clara Farrell returned home at about 11.00pm after watching television with a friend. A neighbour, Mrs Gledhill, saw her return. She went to the house at 11.15pm to ask Mrs Farrel for an evening paper she had borrowed from her earlier.

Apart from Alec Wilkinson Mrs Gledhill was the last person to see Clara Farrel alive.

The *Barnsley Chronicle* reported the proceedings at the inquest, which was opened on Wednesday 4 May:

Charles Henry Farrell, colliery belt man of Bradbury Balk-lane, Wombwell, said that the deceased was his wife. She had left home on Saturday night with a friend to go and see a friend's television. He himself left for work at Wombwell Main Colliery later the same night and there was no one in the house at the time. 'The next thing I heard about my wife' the witness said, 'was when I received a message at the pit about ten minutes to one telling me to come out of the pit as I was wanted urgently at home'. Witness said he went out of the pit, had a bath and then hurried home. When he got to the end of Bradbury Balk-lane he was told by a Police Officer that his wife was dead. 'There were Policemen and Firemen in the street but I don't think the house was on fire at the time,' he said. He was told that his daughter was in hospital. He said that his daughter Maureen had married Alec Wilkinson last August – Barnsley Feast...[The coroner] 'Had there been trouble about the marriage? Were they living together last Saturday?' 'No Sir... They had not been before the magistrates they had just separated on their own.' Asked by the coroner whether his son-in-law ever visited his home the witness replied: 'Not in a friendly way. He came one time after I had gone to work and Mrs Farrell had to call the Police to have him removed.'... A member of the jury asked "Was your wife a quiet woman or had she a bit of a temper?' Farrell replied 'No. We had words like other people but she did not have a quick temper.' Police Sergeant Robert Leslie Gilbertson said that he was called to Bradbury Balk-lane and arrived there at 12.55 am on the morning of Sunday May 1. He said he found the house was on fire and that the Fire Brigade was in attendance... There was no one in the house except the firemen. The deceased had been removed and taken to Barnsley Beckett Hospital...Dr. David Ernest Price said he saw the body of the deceased at 2.30 a.m. on May 1, and again at 4 am. He made a post-mortem examination shortly after 9 a.m. and submitted a short preliminary report.

The post-mortem examination conducted by Home Office Pathologist Dr David E Price revealed that Mrs Farrell's nose was broken. There were deep bruises to the face and either side of the throat suggesting that she had been gripped tightly by the throat during the attack. There was an incised wound across the throat and wounds beneath both her breasts and she had three further wounds of a similar nature on her back, one on the thigh and one on the buttocks. Several minutes into the examination Dr Price discovered a bread knife protruding from the body. This knife had caused injuries to the intestines and had cut into the liver. In addition to the knife found in the body a blood-stained bread knife was found under a cushion at the murder scene and near the kitchen a bloodstained pair of scissors.

Death in Dr Price's opinion was due to shock and haemorrhage following multiple injuries. He said that the wounds on the body were consistent with a knife having being used but he did not think that scissors had been used as a weapon. The injuries to the body caused by kicking and punching were a swelling and bruising of the scalp, forehead and face. Mrs Farrell had blackened eyes, a broken nose, bruising to the chest wall and ten fractured ribs. On the left cheek there were patterned marks consisting of five horizontal stripes equal distances apart that could have been made by a shoe being stamped in her face. Other marks on the body could have been caused by finger pressure, including a broken voice box, small haemorrhage on each side of the lips consistent with pressure on the mouth and bruises beneath each ear. The wounds caused by a knife or another sharp instrument were a three inch long and a one to one and a half-inch deep incision of the throat, which Dr Price described as a 'sawing injury consistent to the wound being caused by a knife with a serrated edge'. There were cuts on the left and right hand sides of the chest and a wound in the lower half of the body. This particular wound he discovered when carrying out the examination. Just an inch of the knife's handle was protruding from the body. The blade had also caused grave internal injuries. As far as burns to the body were concerned Dr Price said he thought most of the burns had occurred after death. There was extensive burning and charring of the right leg and the right side of the body:

I think that the injuries to head and face and possibly the injuries to the neck were sufficient to have made Mrs Farrell unconscious.

The inquest was adjourning pending the result of criminal proceedings.

On Friday 3 June, Alec Wilkinson made his sixth appearance at Barnsley West Riding Magistrates' Court, where he was remanded for a further week in Leeds Prison at the request of Chief Inspector B E Vaughan, prior to the hearing in the same court scheduled for the following week. He was charged with the murder of his fifty-year-old mother-in-law, Clara Farrell. Among the fifty members of the public in attendance at the courthouse for the brief hearing, were Wilkinson's father, mother and two of his sisters. As he left the court handcuffed to a Police officer Wilkinson stopped briefly to speak to his family.

On Tuesday 7 June 1955 the hearing began at Barnsley Court House. On Alec Wilkinson's behalf a plea of 'not guilty' was made by Mr A S McKenzie. He reserved his defence. Outlining the case for the prosecution Mr R L D Thomas acting for the Director of Public Prosecutions. Mr Thomas commented on the newlyweds living close to Mrs Wilkinson's parents and remarked:

> *There seems to be little doubt that Mrs Farrell frequently went into their house trying to assist them as far as she could.*

Throughout the six-hour hearing no sign of emotion was evident on Wilkinson's features. As the pathologist gave his evidence Wilkinson leant forwards and listened intently. He was wearing the same blue suit, white open-necked shirt and red cardigan that he had worn at his six previous court appearances. He whistled silently to himself and periodically played with his heavily nicotine-stained fingers.

Mr Thomas said following his wife returning home to her parents on 20 February Wilkinson went to see her on several occasions. Mr Thomas said:

> *There seems little doubt that by this time he resented the attitude of Mrs Farrell. He did say to one of the neighbours 'It is her. If it wasn't for her me and Maureen would make a go of it.'*

Dr J P Naylor of 39 Broadway, Barnsley said when he saw Mrs Farrell at 1.12am in the casualty ward at Barnsley Beckett Hospital she was dead. Maureen Wilkinson was unconscious.

She had lacerations over her right eye and was bleeding from her right ear.

Dr D R Fry, house surgeon at Beckett Hospital told the court that he examined Mrs Maureen Wilkinson at 9.00am on 1 May and found she had lacerations on the right eye lid, she was bleeding from the right ear and the right nostril and had bruises round her eyes. He suspected she had a fractured skull but an X-ray did not reveal one. Her hair was singed and she remained unconscious for four days. She was discharged from hospital on 18 May and apart from some loss of memory surrounding the events she had made a remarkable recovery.

One witness, Mr Frederick Beavers, labourer, of 24 Doncaster Road, Barnsley was carried into the court room by four policemen. He had earlier been brought to the court house by ambulance from Barnsley Beckett Hospital where he was a patient. He told the magistrates he had known Alec Wilkinson for only a few weeks. On 30 April at 3.15pm he walked with him down Doncaster Road to the *Alhambra Hotel*, where they had a couple of drinks. As they parted Mr Beavers said Wilkinson said to him:

I am going to do somebody in.

Mr Beavers said:

I told him not to be so silly.

Some time later Wilkinson went to the *Wellington Café* at Barnsley. Ronald Norton of Union Street, a part-time help at the café heard Wilkinson tell the manageress, Mrs Evans, that he would not see her again 'next week'. Mr Norton said that he thought Wilkinson had had some beer but he was not drunk. He added that he seemed quite normal. Wilkinson phoned from the café to book a cab, which arrived at about 11.00pm. The taxi took him to Wombwell as far as the *Half Way House*. During the journey he told taxi driver Richard Dorricott of King Street, Barnsley something about 'doing somebody in'. Mr Dorricott said:

He appeared to have had something to drink but I don't think he was drunk.

Wilkinson called at his sister's house in Hammerton Street to ask her to go and see his wife for him but the house was in complete darkness, so he went on to Bradbury Balk Lane himself.

Sometime around midnight Alec Wilkinson attacked his mother-in-law in her home. There were various witness accounts. Mrs Vera Thomson of 70 Hammerton Street, Wombwell said that on the night of 30 April she went with Maureen Wilkinson and Mrs Doreen Keen to a dance at Low Valley. They walked home together and separated when they came to Bradbury Balk Lane. They had only gone a few yards when they heard a scream:

We ran down the street and saw that Mrs Farrell's house was ablaze... I looked in through the front door and I saw a fire in the middle of the room. Maureen was lying on the floor with her feet towards the doorway and her head facing the scullery... I saw Alec Wilkinson standing over her, booting her on the head. He did it three or four times. I shouted at him to stop, but he took no notice. He just carried on and never looked up. I went to a neighbour for help.

Mrs Doreen Keen of 32 Myers Street, Wombwell said she went along to the Farrells' house with Mrs Homson and while Mrs Homson went for help she stayed behind and saw Alec Wilkinson grab hold of his wife by her head and shoulders and bang her head on the floor. She said:

He did it a lot of times.

Neighbour Mr Lewis Taylor of 19 Bradbury Balk Lane said he was awakened soon after midnight by the sound of 'bumping'. He heard a voice that sounded like Alec Wilkinson's and then heard a scream. When he went to the Farrells' house he found Maureen lying on the floor in the blazing room. He picked her up and carried her out onto the pavement, then returned to the house and attempted to get Mrs Farrell out of the house but the heat drove him back. Mr Taylor also told the court that on 30 April he had been sitting at home when he heard banging next door. He heard Alec Wilkinson call out:

I want my wife.

He then heard a conversation between Alec Wilkinson and Mrs

Farrell, who left the house to phone for the police. Mr Taylor said Wilkinson came round to his house and knocked on the door. When he answered it Wilkinson told him he wanted Maureen and said:

It is Mrs Farrell. We would be alright if it wasn't for her.

After this he said nothing. He simply stood there clenching and opening his fists.

Mr Thomas Moore, a miner, of 85 Hammerton Street, Wombwell, was able to get Mrs Farrell's body out of the house by entering through the back door. She was completely naked and he noticed a cut under her right breast. He dragged her into the scullery, covered her with a rug, then carried her to No. 21 Bradbury Balk Lane, the house previously occupied by Alec and Maureen Wilkinson, but now home to new tenants. Maureen was also taken there and both she and her mother were taken from there to Barnsley by ambulance.

PC Gilbertson said that at 12.23am he stopped a patrol car at the top of Bradbury Balk Lane, in which Alec Wilkinson was being taken to the police station. He got in and said that on the journey Wilkinson kept bursting out into fits of laughter. He said:

I have done her in, the old cow. I got the bread knife and stuck her with that. I pulled the furniture round her and just as I was getting it alight the wife walked in so I jumped on her. If she gets over it she will have a stiff neck for a week.

The trial opened on Monday 27 June at Sheffield Assizes before Lord Chief Justice, Lord Goddard. The prosecution was led by Sir Godfrey Russell Vick, QC, the defence by Mr E J Parris. Before the jury of ten men and two women was sworn Lord Goddard listened to a long appeal by the defending counsel to defer the trial for a week. Mr Parris said that the defence were not ready to proceed to trial. He told the judge that information which raised a certain issue were only received last Thursday. Mr Parris said:

On considering this I took the view it was desirable that evidence of the man's mental state should be called. I submit respectfully it is not fair or just to the man that any issue should be left without a most fair and thorough investigation.

Mr Parris said that various psychiatrists had been approached but it had not been possible to obtain one who could examine Wilkinson. He told Lord Goddard:

> *On Saturday I myself went to London to try to find a psychiatrist. In my submission justice cannot be done in this case unless an adjournment is granted. I regret the inconvenience to your Lordship.*

Lord Goddard said the question of inconvenience did not enter into it. He had to consider if it was a proper application to make at that stage. Sir Godfrey Russell Vick, QC, said the prosecution considered it a dilatory application. On the facts the prosecution saw no reason why the trial should not proceed. After listening to further requests by Mr Parris for an adjournment Lord Goddard said:

> *It is now suggested to me that I ought to grant an adjournment. I cannot see any good reason why I should grant an adjournment. The issue of insanity is always on the prisoner, and if his legal advisers want to bring that forward it should have been prepared during the committal proceedings before the magistrates. The first intimation regarding the application for postponement was made to the judge's clerk on Saturday morning. I find it difficult to believe no doctor could be found in Leeds who could have examined the man. The police will help to find other witnesses. The most I can say is that I won't open the defence until tomorrow but the case must proceed.*

Sir Godfrey opened the proceedings for the prosecution by describing the wounds that had killed Clara Farrell as:

> *...horrible and ghastly... The submission of the prosecution that after hearing the evidence the jury will find it abundantly clear that Wilkinson murdered his mother-in-law.*

Mr E J Parris opened the case for the defence on Tuesday 28 June. He said there would be no dispute by the defence that Wilkinson caused Mrs Farrell's death. Neither would the defence be asking for an acquittal. Instead, the defence intended putting forward two matters – the extent of provocation Wilkinson had from his mother-in-law and his state of mind at the time.

Mr Parris said:

> ... *On April 30th he* [Wilkinson] *went to Barnsley, purchasing new shoes, a shirt and a wrist watch. These were not the actions of a man who was intending to do a crime. The defence denies that there had been any premeditation. That day he spent drinking, brooding in misery and 'craving' for his wife. However, he decided to go home to Kendray that night. He was unable to get the last bus home because it was full and so he took a taxi and went to Wombwell instead. On such trivial matters does the destiny of men sometimes depend... On reaching Wombwell he did not go straight to Mrs Farrell's but instead he went to his sister's home in Hammerton Street to ask her to go and see his wife for him. Unfortunately his sister's home was in complete darkness and so he decided on the spur of the moment to go to Mrs Farrell's alone. Driven by nothing more than a craving to see the woman he loved he knocked on the door and went inside... Mrs Farrell was standing in the centre of the room near a table on which was a bread knife. He asked to see Maureen but Mrs Farrell said he could not. Mrs Farrell told him it was true that his wife had left work, and when he asked her how she was going to live Mrs. Farrell replied with the expression implying prostitution and added 'The same as I had to before tha' gets her back.' You can imagine the effect this had on Wilkinson. It was said to him because Mrs Farrell knew it was the most humiliating, scaring and provocative thing she could think of. She then 'flew' at Wilkinson brandishing the knife. She knocked him backwards into the wall and the tip of the knife cut his hand. Wilkinson saw red at this. He struck her down to the floor and he cannot remember anything else after that.*

In referring to the wounds inflicted on Mrs Farrell's body, Mr Parris called the wounds 'symbolical'. They could be explained by Mrs Farrell's comments a short while before. Mr Parris added that in setting fire to the house it was as if Wilkinson was attempting to 'purify' it.

When Alec Wilkinson was called to the witness box it became necessary for Lord Goddard to ask him repeatedly to speak up.

He stared at the floor as he answered questions and five minutes into questioning he began to cry bitterly. He said he was one of twelve children and that his wife, Maureen, had been the only girl in his life. 'I still love her,' he said. He said that Mrs Farrell embarrassed him a lot by making coarse remarks in front of his wife; and he had been given information that led him to believe that Mrs Farrell was not of good moral character. He persuaded Maureen that they should go and live with his mother because he thought Mrs Farrell was an evil influence. Wilkinson told the court:

> *Things went well for a time at Kendray but then we had a sallow row and Maureen went back to her mother's to live. I tried to reach her by sending letters to where she worked but I didn't get a reply.*

He said that on Saturday night he went to see Maureen, arriving at the house at about 11.30pm. Mrs Farrell answered the door and told him Maureen was in bed. He entered the house and went upstairs and found Maureen was not there. Downstairs he picked up a letter written by Mrs Farrell to her son in which Wilkinson said she had written nothing but lies, blaming him for the domestic troubles. With reference to the journey in the taxi from Barnsley to Wombwell, Wilkinson said he did not say to the taxi driver 'He was going to do his mother-in-law in', and added what I said was 'It is enough to make you want her do her in.' He said Mrs Farrell rushed at him knocking him into the wall:

> *She flew at me with the knife and cut me on the hand. I saw red and struck her. The next thing I remember is being upstairs in the house. I remember standing by the bed that Maureen slept in with her mother. I remember thinking that my wife was sleeping with a thing like that. Then I remember flames shooting up.*

During cross-examination by Sir Godfrey Russell Vick, QC, Wilkinson denied setting fire to the house to cover up the crime. He admitted that he disliked Mrs Farrell intensely. He said he was not sorry for what he had done to his mother-in-law but he was sorry for what he had done to his wife. In Wilkinson's evidence it emerged that during one of many quarrels he had with his mother-in-law he had told her that he knew all about her past and why she had the nickname 'The Green Linnet,' to which Mrs Farrell had replied she had been driven to it and began abusing her husband, Charles.

Dr M Jeffreys, consultant psychiatrist at Sheffield City General Hospital, said he thought Mrs Farrell's wounds, if not the tone of the whole crime, were consistent of an action of a man in a schizophrenic episode. When Dr Jeffreys was asked by Lord Goddard if he was prepared to swear that Wilkinson was suffering from a disease of the mind at the time of the crime, Dr Jeffreys replied, 'No.'

In his summing up Lord Goddard referred to a request made by Mr Parris that the charge of murder be reduced to manslaughter on the grounds of provocation and insanity:

> *I must impress upon the jury that in order that a charge of murder be reduced to one of manslaughter the act that caused the death must bear reasonable proportion to the provocation given. You may assume this man's mother-in-law provoked him to some extent, but how could that provocation justify the shocking, horrible and terrible wounds that Wilkinson inflicted upon her...The knife wound had been said by Dr Price, pathologist to have been superficial... Can the wounds inflicted on this poor creature be excused by superficial wounds and words? The dead woman's wounds were enough to make one shudder...As for Wilkinson being insane at the time of the offence. The prison doctor who had Wilkinson under continual supervision since early May, had described him as 'perfectly normal'. True the psychiatrist called by the defence had suggested that the attack could have been committed during a 'schizophrenic episode,' but this psychiatrist had seen Wilkinson only once...*

The jury having considered their verdict returned after fifty-three minutes deliberation with a 'guilty of wilful murder' verdict. Asked if he had anything to say why sentence of death should not be passed on him Alec Wilkinson softly said 'Nothing'. Wilkinson took his arms from the rail as the black cap was placed on Lord Goddard's head. Pronouncing sentence of death Lord Goddard said: 'In all my long life in the law I have never come across such a cruel and dreadful murder.'

An appeal was heard on Monday 25 July. Wilkinson complained that the Lord Chief Justice, Lord Goddard, in his summing up had misdirected the jury as to the burden of proof,

BARNSLEY MAN CHARGED WITH MURDERING HIS MOTHER-IN-LAW

A 21-YEARS-OLD Barnsley miner was charged at Barnsley West Riding Magistrates' Court this week with the wilful murder of his mother-in-law, Mrs. Clara Farrell, of Bradbury Balk-lane, Wombwell, by stabbing her with a knife. The body of the woman was found in the blazing living room of her home: her daughter was also dragged from the burning house in a serious condition.

Dragged through flames

WOMBWELL MURDER CHARGE

Young Barnsley Man to Stand Trial at Sheffield Assizes

GRIM STORY OF DOMESTIC TRAGEDY

AFTER a six hours hearing in a full and hushed Barnsley court room on Tuesday, Alec Wilkinson (21), a miner, of 12, Gerald Walk, Kendray, was committed for trial at the next Sheffield Assizes charged with murdering his mother-in-law, Mrs. Clara Farrell (50), of Bradbury Balk Lane, Wombwell. Wilkinson, represented by Mr. A. S. McKenzie, pleaded "not guilty" to the charge and reserved his defence. He will be defended at Sheffield by Mr. John Parris.

A bread knife in body

DEATH SENTENCE FOR WOMBWELL CRIME

"Cruel and Dreadful Murder" Says Lord Chief Justice

DEFENCE PLEA OF INSANITY FAILS

Wilkinson to appeal

WOMBWELL MURDER CASE: APPEAL FAILS

THE Court of Criminal Appeal on Tuesday dismissed the appeal of Alec Wilkinson (22), miner, of Gerald Walk, Kendray, Barnsley, against his conviction at Sheffield Assizes on a charge of murdering his mother-in-law, Mrs. Clara Farrell, at Bradbury Balk Lane, Wombwell, at midnight on April 30th. He had been sentenced to death.

Wilkinson complained that the Lord Chief Justice (Lord Goddard), in his summing up, had mis-directed the jury as to burden of proof, provocation and insanity.

At the conclusion of submissions by Mr. E. J. Parris, for Wilkinson, the Court did not call on Sir Godfrey Russell Vick, Q.C. to reply for the Crown.

Mr. Justice Hilbery, who sat with Mr. Justice Slade and Mr. Justice Barry, said the law on provocation, reducing murder to manslaughter, had been made clear by the House of Lords. If there was not sufficient material, even on a view of the evidence most satisfactory to the accused for a jury to form the

Mr. Parris said Lord Goddard, in his summing up, did not put certain parts of the evidence accurately to the jury.

Mr. Parris said Wilkinson was separated from his wife, who lived with her mother at Wombwell and he had been forbidden to go there. He went there and there was a fight in which Mrs. Farrell was killed. Wilkinson claimed provocation.

Mr. Parris said the Lord Chief Justice had given no directions to the jury as to the standard of proof required from the prosecution and had misdirected them as to the burden of proof when provocation arose.

EXECUTION DATE

MURDER PETITION

After Attorney-General Rejects Lords Application

LEC WILKINSON (21), miner, of Gerald Walk, Kendray, Barnsley, who is due to be executed at Leeds next Friday for the murder of his mother-in-law, Mrs Clara Farrell, at Wombwell, was told by the Governor of Armley Jail on Wednesday that the Attorney-General, Sir Reginald Manning-ham-Buller, had rejected an application to take the case to the House of Lords.

provocation and insanity. The appeal was held before Mr Justice Hilbery, Mr Justice Slade and Mr Justice Barry. Mr Justice Barry said the law on provocation, reducing murder to manslaughter, had been made clear by the House of Lords. His Lordship continued:

> *In our view, there was no case in law to go to the jury on a question of provocation. In those circumstances it is academic to discuss whether there was sufficient direction to the jury on this point. On the second contention, that there had been insufficient direction on the question of insanity than that given by Mr Parris himself, at the trial, Mr Parris had said the psychiatrists are not saying that this was a schizophrenic episode, but that bears some of the symptoms.*

On Tuesday 26 July the judges of the Court of Criminal Appeal dismissed Alec Wilkinson's appeal. An application was made to the Attorney-General, Sir Reginald Manningham-Buller to take the case to the House of Lords but the application was turned down. An execution date was set for 12 August. On Saturday 6 August the *Barnsley Chronicle* reported:

> *…With just seven days left to make a final bid to save the life of their brother, the Wilkinson family, headed by Alec's father [sixty-nine-year-old Ralph Wilkinson] – there are seven in the family – are making effort this weekend to get every possible signature on a petition which will be presented to the Home Secretary…Organizing the petition is a committee of four Barnsley Main miners headed by Mr Philip Rudd. Mr Rudd said this week: 'I would move every pit heap in the district if it would help Alec, who was one of the most popular men at the pit.' Wilkinson will make his own personal petition to the Home Secretary for his sentence to be commuted.*

The Home Secretary decided there were not sufficient grounds to justify him in recommending any interference with the due course of the law. Alec Wilkinson was hanged at Armley Gaol, Leeds on Friday 12 August 1955 by Steve Wade. His assistant executioner was Robert Leslie Stewart.

CHAPTER 12

The Springfield Street Murder, Barnsley, 1962

...Lily Stephenson had been sexually assaulted then battered to death.

Lily Stephenson was a child prodigy. This brilliantly talented pianist met her husband to be in 1914, when at the age of thirteen she was conducting the orchestra at the Theatre Royal, Durham. In February 1962, sixty-eight-year-old, Albert Stephenson said:

> *I was playing the violin. We were married seven years later and soon afterwards I came down to Yorkshire to work at Barrow Colliery. For the next thirty years I worked at Woolley Colliery but I retired three years ago with chest trouble.*

During World War Two Lily worked for ENSA as a pianist and afterwards was much in demand in pubs and clubs throughout the Barnsley area, where her dexterity on the keyboards earned her good money. At 4.15pm on Tuesday 30 January 1962 Lily left her husband at home at 45 Springfield Street, Barnsley to go shopping at Town End. She carried two shopping bags and was wearing a navy blue overcoat, blue scarf and black fur-lined boots. Now aged sixty-one, Lily stood 5ft 3in tall. She was of slim build, with a fresh complexion and grey, permanently waved hair. When she didn't return home her worried husband reported her missing to police.

At 11.00am the following morning, Wednesday 31 January, Lily Stephenson's body was discovered by Detective Constable Clifford Chatterton in company of Detective Inspector Riley. Mrs Stephenson was in a crouching position wedged in an 18-inches wide gap at the back of and between garages accessed via a 15ft by 4ft yard, just off Springfield Street. Available evidence later suggested that she had been taken to the yard probably by force and sometime later her body had been dumped in the 18-

inches wide alley which ran like the leg of a 'T' from the yard between the two garages, situated less than a hundred yards from the front door of her home. Her two shopping bags were nearby.

The body was taken to the borough mortuary in Eastgate. Home Office Pathologist Dr David E Price, followed by two forensic scientists from the North-Eastern Forensic Laboratory at Harrogate, arrived at the mortuary at 2.00pm to make a detailed examination. Dr Price concluded that Lily Stephenson had been sexually assaulted then battered to death. Three hours later a meeting was convened between Dr Price, the scientists and the Chief Constable, Mr George Parfitt. Afterwards Mrs Stephenson's belongings were taken back to Harrogate for microscopic examination. The discovery of the body led to all police leave in Barnsley being cancelled. A painstaking forensic examination of the crime scene took place and various samples were taken away for analysis.

Albert Stephenson told *Barnsley Chronicle* reporter Robin Morgan in an interview at his daughter, Mrs Constance Heywood's, house at 21 Springfield Terrace:

> *My wife switched the television on for me before going out to buy groceries. She was only going as far as Town End. I made the tea but she did not come. At 8p.m. I told the police she was missing…We were very happily married and this has been a terrible blow to me.*

Lawrence Heywood, Mrs Stephenson's son-in-law, a self-employed window cleaner said she had suffered from pleurisy and pneumonia about eight or nine years previously and since that time she had experienced bouts of chestiness each year. In the past few weeks she had been complaining of breathlessness. He added:

> *She was getting about very steadily but she was never a person to rush about.*

Lily Stephenson was known throughout Barnsley as the 'happy pianist'. She had played regularly at the *Wellington Hotel*. Thirty-seven-year-old railway shunter Fred Greaves of Crown Avenue Cudworth, a committee member at Darfield Road WMC, Cudworth told reporters:

There was always a big demand for Lily Stephenson and she didn't have to go short of work. She used to earn £2 a night here and was very popular with people of all ages. She could play anything from Beethoven to boogie with ease and accomplishment. It's a tragedy that she should have died in such a way.

Police enquiries established that Lily walked from Springfield Street into Dodworth Road and on to Town End to get some groceries and was last seen for certain at about 5.30pm on that dark January evening. She was believed to have been attacked in the half-hour after she had last been seen alive. The discovery of her body sparked the biggest manhunt in Barnsley's history. Under the direction of Scotland Yard officers Detective Superintendent James McKay and Detective Sergeant Ron Ashby, Barnsley borough policeman, working as many as fifteen hours a day took over 3,000 statements and checked the movements of 2,500 men, which led to one principal suspect but no arrest was ever made. In August 1963 a resumed inquest returned a verdict of murder by person or persons unknown. Such was the brutality of Lily's assault and murder that eighteen years later it led one retired police officer to suggest, before the arrest of Peter Sutcliffe, that Lily could have been the first victim of the Yorkshire Ripper.

In March 1984, police announced they had reopened the

case following new evidence. An appeal for information was made by Detective Chief Inspector Albert Pagett, who was in charge of the new investigation. In March 1984 he told the *Barnsley Chronicle*:

> *As a result of new evidence we have re-opened the case and we are looking for several people to help our enquiries. Other police forces have been contacted and enquiries have been made in Preston and in the Midlands... We would like anyone who could help us in our investigation to come forward.*

The investigation suffered a major setback when it emerged that following the reopening of the murder file, as the net appeared to be closing in, a key suspect had disappeared abroad. The man, said to be an Arab, had come to England in the 1950s and had lived in the Monk Bretton area until 1984. Although he was never interviewed in connection with the murder in 1962, shortly after the murder investigation was reopened he fled to Yemen, where despite police efforts to track him down he managed to evade them. In 1992 police spokesman Inspector Barry Stones said:

> *Even after 30 years, if we received any information which we think could lead us to the killer then we wouldn't hesitate to act on it... If the information warranted the re-opening of an incident room, then that is what we would do.*

While police may no longer be making active enquiries concerning what became known as the Springfield Street Murder, they have never closed the case.

CHAPTER 13

Lucky Escape for a Killer, Monk Bretton, 1962

We sized each other up and he said, 'Get tha' back against t' wall because tha's going to need it.' I got at the side of the wall and he swung at me and missed. I dug down and when I came up I hit him in the face with my fist.

On Sunday 11 February 1962, following an incident in the back yard of Barnsley's *Duke of York Hotel*, the town's second murder hunt began within a period of just eleven days. The hunt for the killer of sixty-one-year-old Mrs Lily Stephenson (see Chapter Twelve) was well underway, when news of a second killing hit the streets.

Not long after 10pm on Sunday night, forty-two-year-old housewife Mrs Evelyn Glew of 13 Foster Street, Stairfoot was leaving the *Duke of York Hotel*, by the back door, with a friend, when she came across eighteen-year-old Roy Blakey, lying seriously injured in the back yard. She went back inside the hotel to get help. Mrs Glew said: 'The first thing I saw was a pair of white shirt sleeves. That attracted my attention. Then I saw the boy's body on the ground with blood pouring from his head. His jacket was off and was lying across his knees. He was flat out.' By the time he had arrived at Beckett Hospital, Roy Blakey was already dead.

The *Duke of York Hotel* was situated at 29 Cheapside, at its junction with New Street. It had a distinctive curved façade clad with dark blue tiles to above ground floor window level and light blue tiles up to the roofline. It was one of the town's seedier establishments, which ladies of dubious character were known to frequent. Demolished in 1969, the site is presently occupied by Lloyds TSB Bank.

It was not until quite late on Monday evening that the victim was identified as Roy Blakey. Detective Inspector Harold Riley conducted enquiries. He described the dead youth as being

The Duke of York Hotel, *seen on the left, where Roy Blakey was fatally injured in the back yard on Sunday 11 February 1962.* Chris Sharp of Old Barnsley

dressed 'tidily'. Roy Blakey, a miner, lived at 3 Coronation Street, Monk Bretton. He occasionally drank at the *Duke of York Hotel.* In the early hours of Wednesday 14 February, nineteen-year-old miner, Charles Anthony Dunn, of 21 Baden Street, Worsborough Dale, was charged with Roy Blakey's murder. At 9.40pm on Tuesday 13 February when Dunn returned home to Baden Street, Detective Constable Chatterton was waiting for him. When told by DC Chatterton that he was enquiring into Roy Blakey's death, Dun replied:

Yes, I know. I knew you were looking for me.

In the car on the way to Barnsley Police Station, Dunn said to DC Chatterton: 'What's the most I can get for this? I know you've not got all the evidence yet.' Dunn was distressed and started to cry. His speech was stifled. He uttered the words: 'All's done, everything's finished … All the things I have wanted to do have gone bust… It will kill my mother… Don't tell them… Let them enjoy tonight.' When DC Chatterton asked him what had happened, Dunn said: 'He kept on looking at me.'

He started to cry again, then said: 'Let me settle down and I'll tell you all about it.'

At Barnsley Police Station Dunn told DC Chatterton:

> *You did not expect me to stand still. You have got to, he's a man, so I had a go.*

Detective Inspector Harold Riley who took Dunn's statement asked him if he wished to make any explanation, to which Dunn replied:

> *Yes, he has picked on me for the last fortnight. On Sunday in the 'Duke' he stared at me and I went up to him and said, 'What's up like?' He said 'Tha's handsome' and I said: 'Oh.' He said: 'Do you want to make something of it?' I said I was easy and we went outside. You can't back down because if you do you are blown out of town.*

At this stage Dunn once again became distressed and broke down. Shortly afterwards he calmed down and Inspector Riley took a statement from him in writing.

At 1.05am Detective Inspector Riley charged Dunn. In charging Dunn Inspector Riley said that Charles Anthony Dunn: 'On February 11 1962 at Barnsley did murder Roy Blakey, against the peace of our Sovereign Lady, her Crown and Dignity.' Later that afternoon Dunn was escorted into Barnsley Court House, handcuffed to Detective Constable Clifford Chatterton. Standing 5ft 11in tall, brown-haired Dunn, was dressed in a white shirt, blue sweater and blue jeans. He appeared before magistrate Mr A R Keeping. Superintendent R Harrison said:

> *At 10.10pm on Sunday February 11, a call was received from the Duke of York Hotel, where a man was found in the yard by customers, suffering from head injuries. He died later in Beckett Hospital... As a result of police enquiries the defendant was brought to headquarters at 9.45pm last night [Tuesday] and at 1.00am he was charged with the offence... I am applying for a remand to the police cells until tomorrow, when a further application will be made.*

The magistrates' clerk, Mr Lance Littlefair, then called

Barnsley Chronicle and South Yorkshire News, Saturday, March 10, 1962.

'POINTLESS QUARREL' LED TO DEATH, COURT TOLD

Youth committed for trial at Leeds Assizes

A boy was murdered in the Duke of York Hotel yard because he stared and talked sarcastically at his 19-years-old assailant. This was the reason, alleged Mr. Christopher Bourke, at Barnsley Borough Magistrates Court on Wednesday, why Roy Blakey (18), a miner, of 3, Coronation-street, Monk Bretton, died on February 11.

The Court committed Charles Anthony Dunn (19), miner, 21, Baden-street, Worsbrough Dale, for trial at Leeds Assize, which opens on Monday on a charge of murder.

During the hearing, which lasted five and a half hours, Dunn, who wore a black overcoat, black suit, white shirt, grey, black and white horizontal striped tie and a red sweater, sat between two Police officers occasionally blinking nervously, and listened as 14 witnesses gave evidence.

Mr. J. Donald Driver appeared for Dunn.

Mr. Bourke, for the Director of Public Prosecutions Office, told the magistrates: "On February 11, the defendant appears to have visited several public houses in Barnsley when he came to the Duke of York Hotel, where he had previously spent some time that evening.

"There he got into a very brief and utterly pointless quarrel with Blakey, whom he thought was looking at him unnecessarily.

"Dunn spoke to Blakey, and thought he answered him sarcastically, when Blakey said he thought Dunn looked handsome. The two youths went into the hotel yard by a back door, and Dunn was hit and wounded. The young man took off his jacket and the defendant took off his overcoat.

"Then Dunn felled him with a great blow on the face, and after that, as the injured man lay on the ground, he hit him and stamped on his face and neck."

"He then put on his coat, and left.

"A doctor thinks that there were at least two blows to the head, and two to the body. There is no evidence that the deceased tried to ward off the blows.

"Death was caused not by direct blows, but by asphyxia due to the inhalation of blood, caused by the punches.

"The defendant has been wholly truthful, as far as we know, in admissions which he made to certain neighbours and which he later made to the Police about the events of that night.

"He was interviewed by the Police on the Tuesday evening

following, when he made a statement which explains what took place.

The statement which Mr. Bourke read to the court, said: "I did not know the lad, but I had seen him around town for the last fortnight.

"I did not notice him until he started going around with that girl, Anne Sheard.

"When I have seen him around, he had looked 'daggers' at me. When I have seen him and said 'How do,' to him he ignored me.

"About 9.30 p.m. we went to the Duke and had half a pint, and I saw this lad staring at me. He was sat right back on the backrest of the wall.

"After we had finished our drinks, I said to my mate 'Just a minute Roy, I'm going to see this lad.'

"I went across and asked him: 'Why are you looking at me?'

"He said: 'Nothing pal, as tha's handsome.'

"While he was talking to me he was opening and closing his hands.

"I said: 'What do you want to make of it?'

"I said: 'I'm easy, like. I'm not bothered.'

"He said: 'Let's go for a walk outside'.

The statement went on: "We went out of the back door into the yard and I was in front of him. I expected a stool coming so I went out sharp.

"We sized each other up and then I expected a blow, and I could not see it. His head hit the floor. I don't remember the sound of his head hitting the floor.

"Dunn moved across to him and started putting his foot on him. By the looks of it, I should imagine he went for his face.

"I noticed him doing it three times and I started shouting at him. I was not shouting long before he gave up.

"Dunn looked as if he had lost control of himself.

"Dunn got his overcoat off me and I was left with Blakey's coat which I put over his feet

"On the way to the bus station I think I told Charlie I did not like the idea of using the boot.

"We caught the Worsbrough Dale bus and went home. As we passed the Duke of York we saw a large crowd around the outside.

"He told me he kept quiet and to say nothing about it. Later I spoke to my father and to the Police.

"Dunn was not real drunk, but he would not feel too good. He could walk and speak without difficulty. He and Blakey were in about the same condition."

"Dunn came to see me about

ROY BLAKEY

Coronation-street, Monk Bretton, said he identified his son's body at the Borough Mortuary on Monday, February 12, at 10 p.m.

Dr. David Price, the Home Office pathologist, said he conducted the post mortem examination on Blakey, who was muscular and 5ft. 9ins. tall.

"On the body, whose identity I did not know at the time, there were injuries which were caused by numerous blows to the head.

"In my opinion, the cause of death was concussion following and due to the application of violence to the head, accelerated by asphyxia following and due to inhalation of blood.

"If he had not been knocked out, the asphyxia would probably not have happened."

"In an unconscious patient where there is bleeding from the nose and mouth, there is far greater danger of blood being inhaled, than in a conscious person who can cough and swallow.

"The blows had been mainly to the head. I estimated a minimum of ten to the head and two to the trunk; the two most severe being to the nose and mouth, which broke the nose, upper gum and knocked some teeth out.

"The blows to the head, in the case of those on the right side and front, including the face, had been caused with varying degrees of force, by localised and in some cases, rough surfaces, which could have been fists or footwear.

TWISTED

"The injury which he had to the back of his head, was typical of those produced when the head is struck by, or hits, a hard flat surface. It would not cause death in itself.

"I thought an injury was caused by Blakey's collar and tie being grabbed and twisted sharply and I thought a three inch neck injury was caused by stamping.

"There was no sign that the man had attempted to defend himself."

Dr. Price examined a pair of "winkle picker" type shoes, which were alleged to be Dunn's, and said: "Blows from the toes and heels of these shoes could have caused injury."

He continued: "I examined the defendant on February 14, with his consent, and found some scratches on the back of his right hand over his knuckles, which I thought were about two or three days old."

Mr. Stuart Kind, a principal scientific officer of the Home Office Forensic Science Laboratory at Harrogate, said that Blakey's blood group was "B" and Dunn's "A."

Blood found under Dunn's right shoe was group "B."

Blakey had consumed about five pints of beer that night up to his death.

Mr. James Anthony Pearce, a miner, of 177, Darfield-road,

5.30 p.m. on the Monday and asked if I had heard about this boy. I said 'Yes.'

He said he did not mean to go so far, especially with his boot

"He said he had been to the cinema, where he had been thinking about it and had had a good cry about it. He said he had tried to get down on the sofa but could not sleep, and could not eat through worry.

"He asked me if my mother knew and I said she did. I said we had not been to the Police, but we were very frightened about it.

"Dunn asked me: 'Do you think they will go to the Police?' but I could not reassure him at the time."

Mr. Robert Robinson, colliery deputy, 12, Lang-crescent, Barlton Grange, said that while he was in the hotel toilet about 10 p.m. he heard a voice in the yard outside say: 'Come on now, I think you've done enough.'

He returned to the concert room and two or three minutes later some women ran in. He sent a message for an ambulance and went into the yard, where he saw Blakey.

He helped carry the body into the concert room, where he administered first aid.

"The body was unconscious. He was gasping for breath, the pulse seemed to be weak," he said.

P.C. James Trueman was called to the hotel, where he found Blakey's body lying about eight feet from the hotel entrance. He went with Blakey to the hospital, where death was pronounced at 10.45.

Eileen Whittaker, 10, Elms-dale, said that at 6 p.m. on Tuesday, February 13, a young boy knocked on her door and she saw Dunn on the other side of the road. She went across to have a word with him.

"I told him my husband had been to the Police Station and had reported Charlie for what our Roy had told us on Sunday night.

"I said it was making us all ill and he said he did not see why it should make us ill as Roy had nothing to do with it.

PENETRATED

"Dunn said he smacked him and he dropped. 'And I ought to have realised then for it. He said Roy had nothing to do with it and that Roy had shouted and it sort of penetrated.

"He told him he could not sleep and he could not eat.

"I asked him to have a word with his mother and dad but he said he did not like to as it would hurt them."

D.C. Clifford Chatterton said: "On Tuesday, February 13, I went to 21, Baden-street, Worsbrough Dale, but the defendant was out at that time. I remained at his house and at 9.40 p.m. he returned.

"I told him I was inquiring into Blakey's death. Dunn said: 'Yes, I knew. I knew you were looking for me.'

"I told him we were going to take him to Barnsley Police Station for further enquiries.

"En route in the Police car Dunn said to me: 'What's the most I can get for this. I know you've seen Whittaker, but you've not got all the evidence yet.'

"Dunn was distressed and started to cry and was stilted in his speech. He was saying. 'All done . . . Everything finished . . . All the things I have wanted to do have gone bust . . . It will kill my mother . . . Don't tell them . . . Let them enjoy to-night . . . What can I get for this, what's the most they can give me.'

"I asked him what had happened and he said: 'He kept looking at me'

Barnsley Chronicle

Detective Inspector Harold Riley. Inspector Riley told the court: 'I saw Dunn at 10.00pm and again at 1.00am when I charged him. He made no reply when charged.' When asked if he had any objection to a remand in custody, Dunn replied: 'No'. When asked if he would like legal aid Dunn replied in the affirmative. During the hearing Dunn's father was at the rear of the court. Afterwards he went to the police station where he saw his son.

On Thursday 15 February, the same day, an inquest was opened and adjourned on the body of Roy Blakey by the coroner, Mr Sanderson Gill. Superintendent Harrison applied for Charles Dunn to be remanded to Leeds Prison for one week. Superintendent Harrison said that documents would be sent to the Director of Public Prosecutions for a decision on how matters should proceed.

At the inquest the victim's father, Mr Charles Blakey said that his son went out at 6.40pm on Sunday evening. Mr Blakey told the inquest: 'I was not worried when he did not come home on Sunday evening as he sometimes stayed at his young lady's... But when I heard of the incident on Monday evening, I saw the police and identified his body in the mortuary.' Roy Blakey's girlfriend, Miss Anne Sheard, of Hardwick Crescent, Athersley, was present at the inquest.

Mr George Davies, licensee at the *Duke of York Hotel*, told the inquest:

The boy was brought inside and we tried to give him first aid. I called the police and an ambulance. It had been a very quiet Sunday evening, and we had no trouble at the pub. The boy had not been in that evening. I knew him only as 'Dusty'. He used to come in occasionally and have half a pint by himself.

On Wednesday 7 March, Charles Dunn appeared at Barnsley Borough Magistrates' Court. During the hearing, which lasted five and a half hours, Dunn sat between two police officers. He was wearing a black overcoat, black suit, white shirt, a black and white horizontal striped tie and a red sweater. He occasionally blinked, giving way to nerves as he listened to fourteen witnesses. Mr Bourke appeared for the Director of Public Prosecutions. Mr J Donald Driver appeared for Dunn.

Mr Bourke told the magistrates:

On February 11 the defendant appears to have visited various public houses in Barnsley. He came to the Duke of

York Hotel, *where he had previously spent some time that evening. There he got into a pointless quarrel with Dunn when he thought he was looking at him unnecessarily. Dunn spoke to Blakey, and thought he answered him sarcastically when Blakey said he thought Dunn looked handsome. The two youths went into the hotel yard by a back door and Dunn was hit and wounded. The young man took off his jacket and the defendant took off his overcoat. Then Dunn felled him with a great blow on the face, and after that as the injured man lay on the ground, he hit and stamped on his face and neck. He then put on his coat and left. Death was caused not by direct blows but by asphyxia due to the inhalation of blood caused by the punches. The defendant has been wholly truthful as far as we know, in admissions which he made to certain neighbours and which he later made to police about the events of that night…*

A signed statement made to the police by Dunn was read out in Court:

I did not know the lad but I had seen him around town for the last fortnight. I did not notice him until he started going around with that girl, Anne Sheard…When I have seen him around he had 'looked daggers' at me. When I have seen him and said, 'How do,' to him, he ignored me. About 9.30pm we went back to the 'Duke' and had half a pint and I saw this lad staring at me. He was sat right back on the backrest of the wall. After we had finished our drinks I said to my mate, 'Just a minute Roy, I'm going to see this lad.' I went across and asked him, 'Why are you looking at me?' He said, 'Nothing pal, as tha's handsome.' While he was talking to me he was opening and closing his hands. He said, 'What do you want to make of it?' I said, 'I'm easy like. I'm not bothered.' He said, 'Let's go for a walk outside.' We went out of the back door into the back yard and I was in front of him. I expected a stool coming so I went out sharp. We sized each other up and he said, 'Get tha' back against t' wall because tha's going to need it.' I got at the side of the wall and he swung at me and missed. I dug down and when I came up I hit him in the face with my fist. We must have got close together and we started wrestling. He must have hit me in the stomach because I felt sick. I took my overcoat off and gave it to Roy and while I was taking my overcoat off he must have taken his little coat off. I turned round and hit him straight away. I did not realise he must have been knocked out. He fell straight back and must have hit his head on the ground. I did not know he was unconscious so I went round and hit him in the face once or twice. I didn't really kick him in the face. I brought my foot down on his face. I did not want him to come again. I did not want to disfigure him. I just wanted to hurt him so he wouldn't come again.

Roy Whittaker, a joiner's labourer, of 10 Elmsdale, Worsbrough Bridge gave his evidence regarding Dunn's movements on the night Roy Blakey was fatally wounded:

We went to various pubs in Barnsley and got there [the Duke of York Hotel] *for the second time between 9.45pm and 9.50pm. We got shandies and sat down by the stage where we were talking to the drummer. Dunn had about six and a half pints of beer and shandies that night. Whilst we were talking Dunn got up and told me he would not be a minute. I never looked round to see where he went. The wall clock showed ten o'clock when I got up to go and I left by the back door. I saw Charlie and this boy Blakey in the yard, but I had never seen Blakey before. Dunn was bent over holding his stomach. Blakey was in front of himself cautious and ready. He looked to be on his guard. Blakey said, 'I hope he's not going to start,' and I said 'I want nothing to do with it.' I asked Charlie what had happened and he said the boy had struck him in the stomach. Blakey said, 'Come on then, I'm Ready.' Blakey put his fists up, then he started to take his coat off. He asked me to hold it and I replied, 'I don't want your coat. I don't want anything to do with it.' He seemed to push it on to me, sort of making me have it. Dunn said, 'We might as well be even,' and took his overcoat off. Dunn hit Blakey with what appeared to be the back of his clenched fist. Blakey was not facing Dunn square on, he was a little bit to the side. Before Blakey was hit his fists were at the ready. He toppled over and gave way at the knees and went straight back over and fell down on his back. He went down into a shadow and I could not see if his head hit the floor. I don't remember the sound of the head hitting the floor. Dunn moved across to him and started putting his foot on to him. By the looks of it, I should imagine he went for his face. I noticed him doing it three times and I started shouting at him. I was not shouting long before he gave up. Dunn looked as if he had lost control of himself. Dunn got his overcoat off me and I was left with Blakey's coat which I put over his feet. On the way to the bus station I think I told Charlie that I did not like the idea of using the boot. We caught the Worsbrough Dale bus and went home. As we passed the* Duke of York Hotel *we saw a large crowd around the outside. Dunn's fist was cut along the back and we wiped it with his handkerchief. He told me to keep quiet and to say nothing about it. Later I spoke to my father and to the police. Dunn was not real drunk but he would not feel too good. He could walk and speak without difficulty. Blakey and he were in about the same condition. Dunn came to see me about 5.30pm on the Monday and asked if I had heard about this boy. I said 'Yes.' He said he did not mean to go so far especially with his boot. He said he had been to the cinema where he had been thinking about it and had had a good cry about it. He said he had tried to get down on the sofa but could not sleep and could not eat through worry. He asked me if my mother knew and I said she did. I said we had not been to the police but we were very frightened about it. Dunn asked me, 'Do you think they will go to the Police?' But I could not reassure him at the time.*

James Anthony Pearce, a miner, of 177 Darfield Road, Cudworth, in his evidence told the court he was with Roy Blakey during the evening of Sunday 11 February until Blakey left by the back door with Dunn. Mr Pearce said Blakey had consumed about five pints of beer and he told the court:

We visited various places in Barnsley. We went to the Duke of York Hotel *about 9.45pm. We had two glasses of bitter and went and sat down in the singing room at the side of the stage, in the corner up against the wall. The defendant came up to us. It was the first time I had seen him. I don't know what he said to Roy Blakey, but Roy said to him, 'Tha's not bad looking.' I heard Dunn Say, 'Come on , let's have you outside.' That's all I can remember of the conversation. They went outside by the back door. Roy went out first, I think. It was about two minutes before time was called at 10.00pm. I went to the toilet and on my way back I saw a woman coming in screaming. This was about four or five minutes after the two had walked out. I went back to the table, supped my drink and went outside by the side door which leads to the yard. There were a lot of people round Roy's body, which was lying on the ground. There was a lot of blood on his face. I was very shocked and distressed and I didn't know what to do, so I went and caught the 10.15pm bus home. The next day I heard of a man's death at the* Duke of York Hotel *and I went to the police. I first told them that Roy had left the Wine Shades and had left me sitting there at 9.30pm, but in my second statement to the police I told them what had happened in the pub.*

Home Office Pathologist Dr David Price carried out a post-mortem examination on the deceased, who at the time had yet to be identified. The deceased was of muscular build and was 5ft 9in tall. Dr Price said:

…there were injuries which were caused by numerous blows to the head. In my opinion the cause of death was concussion following and due to the application of violence to the head accelerated by asphyxia following and due to inhalation of blood…. If he had not been knocked out the asphyxia would probably not have happened. In an unconscious patient where there is bleeding from the nose and mouth there is far greater danger of blood being inhaled than in a conscious person who can cough and splutter. The blows had been mainly to the head. I estimated a minimum of ten to the head and two to the trunk, the two most severe being to the nose and mouth, which broke the nose, upper gum and knocked some teeth out. The blows to the head in the case of those on the right side and front including the face, had been caused with varying degrees of force, by localised and in some cases, rough surfaces, which could have been fists or footwear. The injury which he had to the back of his head was typical of those produced when the head is struck by, or hits a hard flat surface. It would not cause death in itself. I thought an injury was caused by Blakey's collar and tie being grabbed and twisted sharply and I thought a three-inch neck injury was caused by stamping…

Dr Price examined the shoes Dunn was alleged to be wearing at the time of the incident and concluded:

Blows from the toes and heels of these shoes could have caused injury… I examined the defendant on February 14 with his consent and found some scratches on the back of his right hand over his knuckles, which I thought were about two or three days old.

Evidence was also presented by Mr Stuart King, a principal scientific officer of the Home Office Forensic Science Laboratory at Harrogate. Mr King said that Roy Blakey's blood was group 'B' and Charles Dunn's blood was group 'A'. Blood found under Dunn's right shoe was group 'B'.

Dunn gave no evidence and reserved his defence for his trial. He was granted a Defence Certificate for two counsel and an application by Mr Bourke on a thirty guinea fee was allowed. At the end of the proceedings Charles Anthony Dunn was committed for trial at Leeds Assizes.

On Tuesday 10 April 1962, nineteen-year-old Charles Anthony Dunn, stood in the dock at Leeds assizes before Mr Justice Streatfield, dressed in a black suit, white shirt, black and white striped tie, and red sweater. During his trial he only uttered two words. This was towards the end of the proceedings when the clerk asked Dunn if he had anything to say why he should not be sentenced, Dunn replied: 'No Sir.' Dunn was fortunate from the beginning of his trial, the prosecution having accepted his plea of 'guilty' to 'manslaughter'.

Mr Alistair Sharpe, QC, outlined the case for the prosecution:

> *On Sunday February 11, in a yard outside the* Duke of York Hotel, *a youth called Roy Blakey lost his life as a result of a fight with the prisoner.*

Detective Inspector Harold Riley, who had arrested Dunn and charged him with murder, told the court Dunn's past history. He said that Dunn, who would be twenty in June, was educated at local schools and left at the age of fifteen to become a lorry driver's mate. He worked in the pit as a screen and haulage hand, and joined the merchant navy, serving for one trip to South Africa as a deck-hand. Later, while working for British Railways at Sheffield, he was dismissed after assaulting two coloured workmates. He was fined £25 for unlawful wounding and £25 for causing actual bodily harm at Sheffield Sessions. In November 1961 he went back to mining, as a development worker. Inspector Riley, in referring to Dunn's character told the court:

> *He is a person who likes to boast and show his strength with fellow workers...*

The leader of Dunn's defence, Mr Rudolph Lyons, QC, asked of Inspector Riley:

Unfortunately, in this area of Barnsley, a good deal of physical violence takes place?

To which Inspector Riley replied:

Yes.

The judge added:

I'm afraid Barnsley is not the only place where kicking is indulged in.

Mr Lyons then asked the question:

Young men in that area don't seem to appreciate how dangerous it can be?

To which Inspector Riley replied:

I think that is true sir.

Mr Lyons, making his speech for Dunn said:

Rarely could a quarrel leading to a man's death have had such a trivial and absurd reason as this one. Right until Blakey was knocked to the ground, there was very little to choose between the two contestants. Both men probably had more to drink than was good for them. The accused has been brought up in surroundings where fighting is not frowned upon. The fight started as a wrestling match, but the wrestling ended with Dunn being struck a blow in his stomach. It made him feel sick and he fell down. The deceased made to kick at his face, and missed. He is full of contrition and had probably learned his lesson, which he will not forget.

Mr Justice Streatfield told Dunn:

Throughout the length and breadth of the country young people are giving way to violence, and one of the most disgraceful kinds of violence is kicking a man - kicking a man when he is down…It seems to be a kind of pastime, and this sort of thing will not be tolerated…This man died and you were charged with murder…One of the features of this case has been the very small and trivial beginning. But when you had knocked this man down unconscious, you lost your temper and you belaboured him with your fists and began stamping on his face which is one of the most contemptible things a man can do. That man's life is on your hands. You are only 19, and it is that fact which deters me from sending you to prison for a long time.

The judge sentenced Dunn to four years imprisonment.

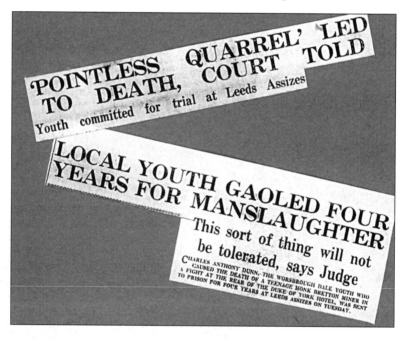

Chapter 14

Acts of Violence by Demolition Worker Ends in Tragedy, Wombwell, 1962

In this country a man is not punished for the result of his act but only for the evil in the act.

At 1pm on Saturday 15 April 1962, thirty-four-year-old Darfield Main Colliery miner, Randle Summers, of 32 Roebuck Street, Wombwell was enjoying a drink in the tap-room of the *Railway Hotel* at Wombwell. He was a bachelor who lived with his parents, Mr and Mrs Jack Summers and was the youngest son of a family of two sons and four daughters. His thirty-six-year-old brother, Jack, of Hatfield Street, Wombwell also worked

A present day view of the Railway Hotel, *Wombwell, where Randle Summers was fatally injured on Saturday 15 April 1962.* The Author

at Darfield Main. Their father was a retired collier. Twenty minutes after his arrival in the *Railway Hotel* Randle Summers was playing a game of whist with twenty-nine-year-old labourer Thomas William Parr, of 92 Netherwood Road, Wombwell and two other men. Events that immediately followed that game of cards during which Summers made a remark to Parr about his wife, resulted in tragedy. Randle Summers was not by nature a fighting man but he did have a reputation for making sarcastic remarks. His last sarcastic remark ultimately cost him his life.

Half-way through the game of whist, according to Parr in a statement made to police, Summers allegedly said within earshot of other drinkers:

> *You don't know your wife like you should – you want to get to know her better.*

Parr had married on 12 November 1960. This remark made by Summers seemed to imply that Parr's wife was not of good character and it rankled Parr as his wife was of perfectly good character. The game continued and Parr said nothing to Summers about the remark. He simply bided his time. Unlike Summers, Parr was a fighting man and he had a reputation for violence. In fact he had a criminal record. Almost eight years previously, on 6 September 1954 he was fined £5 at Barnsley West Riding Court for unlawful wounding and £10 by the same Court on 25 May 1959, for inflicting grievous bodily harm and assault occasioning actual bodily harm. He had had earlier brushes with the law when at the age of ten, twelve and fourteen years, he had committed offences. In July 1953 he was fined for disorderly conduct on a public service vehicle and in December 1953 for wilful damage to drinking glasses and a stool. More recently Parr had committed an offence in the *Railway Hotel,* where his altercation with Summers was to take place. Three years previously Parr had not been satisfied with the result of a talent contest held at the *Railway Hotel* and he had gone over to a table upturned it spilling beer, then he had thrown a stool causing grievous bodily harm. For that offence he had been fined £10.

After what was to be Summers' last game of whist on that fateful Saturday in April 1962 Parr thought about what Summers had said to him and as he commented later: 'The words ate into him.' Neither Summers nor Parr could have been considered to be under the influence of drink. They were used to drink. Parr had visited three other public houses in Wombwell before he entered the *Railway Hotel* and had consumed four pints of beer. Having brooded for a while, Parr struck at Summers but the blow missed him. A scuffle and fight ensued and witnesses said Parr struck Summers about three times. A man named Brook intervened and Parr and Summers were pushed apart and told to stop fighting. They did so and all appeared to be over. The two men sat down. Parr had his back to a window and Summers had his back to a table. Suddenly, Parr struck Summers full in the face. It was a powerful blow, its force knocked Summers backwards over the table. As he fell the table turned over so that it was upside down and Summers' legs were in a position over the step under the table. He was groaning and his head was bleeding. As he had fallen his head had struck the concrete floor. Witnesses later told police that immediately following the incident Parr said:

Don't call my wife.

Randle Summers was taken by ambulance in a half-conscious state to Barnsley to Beckett Hospital, where he was found to have a cut on his lip and one on his scalp. The fractured skull that was to cause his death was not at this stage detected, even though an X-ray was taken. As his condition grew worse he was transferred in an unconscious state to Sheffield Royal Infirmary on Sunday morning, where an immediate emergency operation was carried out. Once again the fracture to Summers' skull was not revealed during the operation.

Meanwhile, police officers visited Parr at 3.55pm. When they arrived he said he had expected them. He made a voluntary statement and was charged with inflicting grievous bodily harm. Unlike Summers Parr had no injuries. On Monday 17 April, at 5pm Randle Summers died of his injuries. When police visited Parr at home at 5.55pm he clearly feared the worst when he said he hoped they weren't going to tell him what he thought. When he was told of Summers' death Parr said: 'Oh dear' and put his head on the mantelpiece and was apparently in a distressed state. He was charged with manslaughter.

On Tuesday 18 April, Parr appeared at a special sitting at Barnsley West Riding Court. Chief Inspector Roland Cusworth told examining magistrate Mr Albert Mason:

LABOURER CHARGED WITH MANSLAUGHTER

A 29-YEARS-OLD Wombwell demolition labourer was charged with manslaughter at Barnsley West Riding Court on Tuesday, following a fight in a local public house with another Wombwell man, two days earlier.

Charged, and in custody, until next Wednesday is Thomas William Parr, (29), 92 Netherwood-road, Wombwell.

The dead man is Randle Summers, aged 34, a miner of 32, Roebuck-street, Wombwell.

At a special sitting of the court, on Tuesday, Chief Inspector Roland Cusworth told the examining Magistrate, Mr. Ilbert Mason: "At 2.30 p.m. on Sunday April 15 the police at Wombwell were called by telephone to the Railway Hotel, Wombwell.

"P.C. Newton and Sergeant Child saw the deceased, who was being carried by ambulance men to an ambulance.

"He was unconscious and was suffering from head injuries.

"He was taken to Barnsley Beckett Hospital."

The Chief Inspector alleged: "In the tap room of the hotel the deceased had been in an argument with the prisoner. The prisoner had hit him with his fists, knocked him over a table and the deceased hit his head on the terrazzo floor.

"The prisoner was arrested by the police and bailed to appear before this Court at a later date.

"The deceased was in Barnsley Beckett Hospital, but his condition deteriorated and he was transferred to the Sheffield Royal Infirmary on Sunday where an emergency operation was performed.

"He died there at 5 p.m. yesterday (Monday).

"At 5.50 p.m. yesterday the prisoner was re-arrested and charged with feloniously killing and slaying Randle Summers.

"The prisoner asked P.C. Newton, when he was charged: 'When shall I appear before the Court? I want my wife to arrange for a solicitor for me'," said the Chief Inspector.

Mr. Doug'as Kemp, appearing for Parr, successfully applied for legal aid for the committal proceedings.

He said Parr was a married man with a fifteen-months-old child and lived with his mother and father.

Summers, a bachelor, lived with his parents, Mr. and Mrs. Jack Summers, at their council house home in Roebuck-street.

He was the youngest son of a family of two sons and four daughters, and worked at Darfield Main Colliery, where his brother Jack, aged 36, of Hatfield-street, Wombwell, also worked.

His father is a retired collier.

RANDLE SUMMERS

Sent for trial to Sessions

A Barnsley road haulier was committed to take trial at the Quarter Sessions by Barnsley Borough Magistrates on a charge of uttering a forged driver's record.

He was John Truelove, 163, Park-grove, Barnsley, who was allowed bail in the sum of £25.

Mr. A. Myerson, prosecuting, said the defendant employed, as one of his drivers, a man named Wales. It was a duty of the drivers, he said, to keep records of journeys and rests and, if they did not do this, they and their employers were liable to commit offences under the Road Traffic Acts.

He said the charge, for which he asked Truelove to take trial at the Quarter Sessions, arose out of a journey undertaken by the man Wales from Barnsley to Ipswich last July.

Mr Myerson said in October last year, Mr. Thomas Millicheap, a traffic inspector, visited Mr. Truelove and asked him for drivers' records which the defendant promised to let him have the following day.

When these were handed to him one of the work sheets showed Mr. George Merrils, of Engine-lane, Shafton, had driven from Barnsley to Ipswich.

But, said Mr. Myerson, when Mr. Merrils was seen it was revealed he had never been employed by the defendant nor driven a lorry for him.

He alleged Mr. Merrills had been asked by Truelove to write out the record sheet as he was short of one. He was told what to write and signed it as the person who had driven the lorry.

Mr. Myerson said that in a statement made by Truelove, he was alleged to have said he got Merrils to write the record sheet because he wanted to keep Wales out of trouble for going over his hours.

Waiter's lip cut by blow

A public house waiter had to have four stitches inserted in a wound in his lip after being struck on the mouth by a 44-years-old unemployed Kendray man, it was stated at Barnsley Borough Court.

Before the Court charged with inflicting actual bodily harm on the waiter, Dennis Bridge, Birk-road, Kendray, was Stanley Bradder, 43, Thornton-road. He pleaded guilty and was fined £5.

Mr. John Peters said Bridge, who was 36, was usually employed as a miner but worked part-time as a waiter at the Junction Hotel.

On February 2 the defendant and his brother Jack went into the public house and were served with drinks by Bridge.

Jack Bradder paid for the drinks with a £1 note and, said Mr. Peters, Bridge was quite sure he gave him the change from the note.

But later in the evening Jack Bradder alleged Bridge had not given him the change.

Mr. Peters said after the defendant had shouted across the bar to the waiter: "You will have to give him the change." Bridge walked over to their table to explain he had given the correct change and there was nothing else he could do.

It was while he was standing over the table, said Mr. Peters, that Bridge was struck a violent blow on the mouth with defendant's fist.

His top lip was very badly cut and he had to go to hospital where four stitches were inserted in the wound.

Mr. Peters said the exchange between Bridge and Jack Bradder had nothing to do with the defendant and he was just interfering in something which did not concern him.

Mr. D. A. Kemp (for Bradder) said Bridge became very excited and said the defendant and his brother were not getting any money from him.

Bradder thought his brother was being cheated out of the money and lost his temper. He struck Bridge because he thought he was going to be struck first.

Mr. Kemp said his client did not intend cutting the other man's lip and he now knew it was a ring he was wearing which caused the cut.

COURT BRIEFS

REMANDED.— Alfred Yeomans (53), unemployed, of no fixed abode, was remanded in custody until to-day (Thursday) by Barnsley Borough Magistrates on Tuesday, charged with being a reputed thief loitering with intent to commit a felony.

SPEEDING.— Said to have driven along Wakefield-road, Barnsley, at 40-45 miles per hour, Norman Chappel, salesman, of 81, Wingfield-crescent, Athersley, was fined £3 and had his licence endorsed by Barnsley Borough Magistrates on Tuesday, for exceeding the speed limit.

BOY FINED. — Whilst a Smithies man was discussing storm damage with a neighbour a potato came through his front room window, Barnsley Borough Juvenile Court heard on Tuesday. An 11-years-old boy was fined 20s. for causing wilful damage to the window, and 20s. for causing wilful damage to a window in Forrest-road, Athersley, in October. In that case, the boy threw a stone and broke a back room window. He had to pay 19s. 8d. damages and costs.

FOUR FINED.— A policeman on duty at Ardsley, heard voices coming from the railway sidings, and saw four youths pushing a potato off wheels along one of the tracks, Barnsley Borough Juvenile Court heard, when the four, aged between 12 and 15, were fined 20s. each for railway trespassing.

FINED 20s.— Said to have left his van parked in Peel-street, Barnsley, for an hour and a half, John Stockley, manager, Parkgrove, Barnsley, was fined 20s. by Barnsley Borough Magistrates, for causing unnecessary obstruction.

NO RECORDS. — Edwin Legard (26), salesman, Granville-place, Barnsley, was fined a total of 30s. by Barnsley

CAUSED OBSTRUCTION. — Geoffrey Blackburn (32), of 43, Linton-crescent, Leeds, was fined 20s. by Barnsley Borough Magistrates on Tuesday, after admitting causing unnecessary obstruction with a motor car.

FINED 50s.— A 24-years-old driver, Alan Gamwell, 63, Ollerton-road, Athersley Estate, was fined a total of 50s. by Barnsley Borough Magistrates on Monday, when he admitted, by letter, using a motor cycle with an inefficient warning instrument, with inefficient brakes and without a test certificate.

OBSTRUCTION. — Arthur Goodwill, 47, Victoria-street, Clayton West, was fined 20s. by Barnsley Borough Magistrates on Monday, when he admitted, by letter, to causing unnecessary obstruction when he parked his car in Shambles-street.

SPEEDING.— Geoffrey Pickering (24), miner, 20, Princess-street, Barnsley, was fined £3 and had his licence endorsed by Barnsley Borough Magistrates for exceeding the speed limit, which he admitted by letter. Supt. R. S. Harrison said a check of the speed of the defendant's car was made over a distance of eight-tenths of a mile in Wakefield-road when speeds varying between 45 and 50 miles an hour were recorded.

REMANDED.— Eric Leighton (40), waiter, 43, Tyldesley-road, Blackpool, was remanded on bail in the sum of £50 self and surety until May 8 by Barnsley Borough Magistrates. He is accused of stealing radios etc., value £550.

Hit lorry on bend

Sheep's heads were scattered over the road at Low Barugh when a butcher's van collided with a lorry on a double bend

OVERWHELMING! —
Independently audited (A.B.C.) readership of the Barnsley Chronicle has now reached over 42,000 copies weekly ....NEWS-AGENTS CERTIFY overwhelming mastery of Chronicle sales....it goes into OVER 82% MORE HOMES than any other medium coming into the Barnsley area.

THE CHEAPEST SMOKELESS FUEL

At 2.30pm on Sunday April 15 the police at Wombwell were called by telephone to the Railway Hotel, *Wombwell...PC Newton and Sergeant Child saw the deceased, who was being carried by ambulance men to an ambulance. He was unconscious and was suffering from head injuries. He was taken to Barnsley Beckett Hospital. In the tap room of the hotel the deceased had been in an argument with the prisoner. The prisoner had hit him with his fists, knocked him over a table and the deceased hit his head on the terrazzo floor. The prisoner was arrested by the police and bailed to appear before this court at a later date. The deceased was in Barnsley Beckett Hospital but his condition deteriorated and he was transferred to the Sheffield Royal Infirmary on Sunday where an emergency operation was performed. He died there at 5pm yesterday. At 5.50pm yesterday the prisoner was re-arrested and charged with feloniously killing and slaying Randle Summers. The prisoner asked PC Newton when he was charged: 'When shall I appear before the Court? I want my wife to arrange for a solicitor for me.'*

Mr Douglas Kemp appeared for Parr and successfully made an application for legal aid for the committal proceedings.

Thomas William Parr made his final appearance before magistrates at Barnsley West Riding Court on Monday 7 May charged that he did 'feloniously kill and slay' Randle Summers on April 15 1962. Mr Maurice Shaffner prosecuting opened the proceedings and said when Parr heard a remark about his wife, the words 'ate into him' and when he finished the game of cards he struck the man who made the remark. Mr Shaffner later said the remark was to the effect that Parr should watch his wife. Parr did nothing about it straight away, but he must have thought about it and it boiled up inside him, for soon after the game Parr struck Summers. Mr Shaffner went on to say that after Randle Summers' death Parr was arrested on a charge of manslaughter. Having outlined the alleged comment made by Summers and having heard witness evidence Mr Shaffner said that remarks made against Parr's wife were completely without foundation. At the conclusion of the hearing Parr was committed for trial at Sheffield Assizes. An application for bail by Parr's solicitor Mr D A Kemp was refused.

The trial of Thomas William Parr was held at Sheffield's May Assizes before Mr Justice Roskill. He pleaded guilty to the charge of manslaughter. Mr Harold S Pears prosecuted and Mr

LABOURER CHARGED WITH MANSLAUGHTER

A 29-YEARS-OLD Wombwell demolition labourer was charged with manslaughter at Barnsley West Riding Court on Tuesday, following a fight in a local public house with another Wombwell man, two days earlier.

COMMITTED FOR TRIAL AT SHEFFIELD ASSIZES

A remark about his wife 'ate into him,' Court is told

WHEN A 29-YEARS-OLD WOMBWELL LABOURER HEARD A REMARK ABOUT HIS WIFE, THE WORDS "ATE INTO HIM" AND WHEN HE FINISHED A GAME OF CARDS HE STRUCK THE MAN WHO MADE THE REMARK, MR. MAURICE SHAFFNER ALLEGED AT BARNSLEY WEST RIDING COURT ON MONDAY.

GAOLED THREE YEARS FOR MANSLAUGHTER

'No mitigating factors,' says judge

THREE years after being fined by Barnsley West Riding Magistrates for offences of violence in the Railway Hotel, Wombwell, Thomas William Parr, 29-years-old demolition worker, Netherwood-road, Wombwell, was sent to prison for three years at Sheffield Assizes on Tuesday, for killing a man in the same hotel.

J M McLusky defended. As well as eyewitness evidence which described the events leading up to the fight and its aftermath the court heard that following Randle Summers' death despite no fracture being evident at the examinations made on his live body at both Beckett Hospital and Sheffield Royal Infirmary, during a post-mortem examination it was revealed there was an extensive fracture of the base of the skull, 5½ inches long. The brain was extensively bruised under the fracture. The injuries were consistent with Summers' head having struck the concrete floor of the tap-room and even if the fracture had been discovered earlier nothing could have been done to save him. Police Constable Neville Newton of the West Riding Constabulary outlined Parr's previous convictions. When he mentioned Parr's last conviction for a violent offence also committed at the *Railway Hotel*, the judge commented:

> *He was fined a total of £10 by the magistrates. That was three years ago. He is now back, charged with killing a man in the same public house.*

Police Constable Newton replied:

> *That is so, my Lord.*

Mr McLusky, defending said:

> *It is a very tragic case. Not only for the victim but also for my client. One could not imagine a more offensive remark being made about his wife... A witness had told the magistrates Summers was sarcastic and would not let a subject drop but kept on about it. He is dead and I don't like speaking against his memory, but he was given to sudden sarcastic remarks...In this country a man is not punished for the result of his act but only for the evil in the act.*

Before sentencing Parr on Tuesday 29 May Mr Justice Roskill told him:

> *You have killed a man with a vicious blow, true, after he had made an insulting remark, but nevertheless in circumstances which cannot be excused... It is not the first time you have been convicted of an act of violence. Only three years ago you were convicted of two acts of violence in the same public house. I can find no mitigating circumstances at all.*

Parr was sentenced to three years imprisonment.

CHAPTER 15

Convicted Sex Offender Rapes and Kills Teenager, Pilley, 1972

I have committed an irrevocable act. I have taken the life of an innocent child. Oh God, I have wanted to tell you all night.

Fourteen-year-old Shirley Ann Boldy lived with her parents Norman and Edna in a semi-detached house in Hemingfield Road, a leafy thoroughfare adjacent to Wombwell Wood that ran from Wood Walk, Wombwell into Hemingfield. Her father was Deputy Housing Manager with Hoyland UDC. Her older brother, Simon, aged twenty-two, was taking a degree in Spanish at Cambridge. Shirley had every reason to feel pleased with herself. She had come top of her class and her end of term report read:

Always gives her best. Shirley should do well next year.

Shirley's headmaster at Wombwell High School, Mr Frank Betts, said of her:

She was a delightful girl who worked hard and was really beginning to prove herself in the classroom.

Deputy Head Mr Eric Middleton commented:

She liked her work and got on with both staff and pupils alike. She was more quiet and retired than the reverse.

On Thursday 13 July 1972, Shirley, an attractive, slimly-built girl, with long blonde hair, finished her morning lessons at Wombwell High School and set off home for lunch. Fellow pupil, fourteen-year-old Ian Morris, of Hough Lane,

Wombwell, accompanied her part of the way before they split up to go to their own homes. Ian said, on Friday 14 July:

I thought the world of her. We had been going steady for about two months...We went to a school dance together earlier this week and we used to go for walks with her dog, Dido.

After having lunch and kissing her mother goodbye, Shirley set off back for school. She was wearing a blue and white cotton dress and cardigan, white socks and sandals and carried a satchel. She habitually went back to school with a group of friends but on that particular day it was not to be the case. Shane Moore, of Quest Avenue, Hemingfield, had been in the same class as Shirley since junior school. That day he had stayed at school for lunch. Another friend was visiting the Great Yorkshire Show and a third, who would normally have been with Shirley had gone back to school early. Shane said:

Normally there would have been three or four of us with Shirley. We used to wait for each other near the farm... Any other day there would also have been a lot of smaller children nearby, but on this day they held their sports day...Shirley was a quiet, home-loving girl. She liked nothing better than hiking with her family or her dog...She was due to move up into the top stream next term because she had come top of her class. She wanted to be a teacher.

Shirley never arrived at Wombwell High School for the afternoon classes on that penultimate day of the academic year. At about three o'clock the same afternoon, about seven miles away, three men were at Barnburgh Cliff when they saw a white mini-van reverse into a gap in the cliff side, at a spot frequently used by courting couples. As they passed by they saw through the van's back window the lower half of a girl's body naked up to the waist except for a pair of white socks and sandals. They also saw a man moving about in the vehicle. He was wearing gloves and held a knife. They heard a scream and saw the girl's legs kick and shake. The van then sped off almost running the men down. One of them threw a stick at the van while another banged on the roof. The other man took down the vehicle's registration number and they reported what they had seen to police. That evening, at 8.35pm, a man was arrested in Wombwell in possession of the mini-van.

When Shirley failed to return home at teatime her parents at first thought she might be attending a music concert. However, after checking with the school, her father reported her missing to police. Shirley's body was found after a massive twelve hour search by over 100 police officers using tracker dogs. They worked throughout the night and searched woodland in the Wombwell, Marr and High Melton districts before the search was switched to Pilley Woods, Pilley Hill, Tankersley, the following morning after revelations were made by the man in custody.

Peter Joseph Wilson Pickering aged thirty-four appeared in the dock at the Doncaster West Riding Court on Saturday 15 July charged with the murder of Shirley Ann Boldy of Hemingfield on 13 July. Pickering wept throughout the four-minute hearing. He was remanded in custody until Friday 21 July. While in custody Pickering told police he was a Buddhist and a man of peace.

Detective Chief Superintendent Donald Craig, head of West Yorkshire CID, said shortly after Shirley's body was discovered:

We want to interview anyone who might have seen her.

An inquest was opened on Tuesday 18 July at Wortley RDC offices. Evidence regarding Shirley's identity was given by her uncle, Mr Thomas Boldy, of Wainwright Avenue, Wombwell. He told the coroner, Dr Albert Pilling, that he had identified the body at Barnsley Public Mortuary on Friday 14 July. In adjourning the inquest Dr Pilling said:

I am going to issue a burial order and adjourn this inquest. I have been informed that someone has already been charged with causing her death.

A private funeral service was held for Shirley on Friday 21 July at Wombwell Parish Church, St Mary's, and afterwards she was laid to rest in the peaceful little cemetery between Hemingfield and Jump.

On Friday 21 July, Pickering appeared again before magistrates at Doncaster West Riding Court. Prosecuting solicitor Stuart Robertson told magistrates that Pickering had told police on the morning of Friday 14 July:

Shirley's grave. The Author

I have committed an irrevocable act. I have taken the life of an innocent child. Oh God, I have wanted to tell you all night.

Mr Robertson told the court that Pickering had then taken police to a lonely spot in Pilley Woods and shown them the whereabouts of Shirley's body. He had also taken them to a spot in Hemingfield where he had abducted her and to a spot at Billingley where he had raped her; then to the place at Barnburgh Cliffs where he had killed her. Mr Robertson added that a post-mortem examination had revealed that Shirley had been strangled and stabbed. Acting for the prisoner, Mr Ralph Cunliffe said he had no objection to a remand in custody. He added:

This man is ill and being kept in a prison hospital, and has no complaint about his treatment.

Peter Pickering, now aged thirty-five, appeared in the dock at Sheffield Crown Court in December 1972 before Mr Justice MacKenna. Mr Barry Mortimer prosecuted and Mr Geoffrey Baker, QC, defended. The court heard that Pickering picked Shirley up as she took a short cut to school across a field. He forced her in his van and tied her hands behind her with twine and drove her to a remote spot in Howell Wood, Billingley about seven miles away, where he ripped off her clothes and brutally raped her. Afterwards he drove around with Shirley still tied up in the back of his van. Eventually he arrived at a spot near the village of Clayton, situated south east of Grimethorpe on the road to Hooton Pagnell. It was then he decided to kill her and silence the only witness. After driving some more, he pulled up at a remote spot. He first tried to strangle Shirley with his hands but then untied her and used the twine to do the job, before he finally plunged a kitchen knife into her heart. While he was doing so he was spotted by three men out walking and as he drove away his vehicle's registration number was noted. This led to Pickering being quickly found and arrested.

In a feeble attempt to explain his deplorable behaviour, he tried to excuse himself on two counts. He said he had desperately sought psychiatric help and been refused it while serving sixteen years in jail for sex offences. Secondly, he blamed his mother for his actions. Pickering said in court:

My mother is to blame for all this. She has possessed me…She would never let me have another woman and always tried to destroy any relationship I had with other females…It was my mother I was killing. I could see my mother when I was doing it. They knew I would do this when I left prison… I nearly cured myself and in a short time I would have been cured but something snapped when I saw the girl walking across a field… The biggest feeling I had was not elation. It was just a feeling of destroying my mother…I have mentioned over the years I wanted help I know I am ill…I have tried to the best of my ability to act as a normal human being I feel nothing but remorse for what I have done…I was in an indescribable mood from which I have always been able to hold myself in check. But this time I felt like exploding…She mentioned something about her mother and something snapped inside me. I tore the clothes off her. I was out of my mind…The least I can do is keep the girl's good name. She fought hard and never asked for any of this. She was a pure girl…

Prosecuting counsellor, Mr Mortimer, told the judge:

The facts of the case are quite the worst and most appalling I have ever had to do with and I dare say they will come high in that way with your Lordship…They were sub-human acts that could only be described as the acts of a monster.

Mr Baker said his client's pleas for psychiatric help during his long years in prison went unanswered. The prosecution accepted Pickering's plea of guilty of manslaughter due to diminished responsibility. Mr Mortimer said that the offences had been committed only five months after Pickering had been released from a nine-year jail sentence for indecent assault and causing grievous bodily harm to a girl. He had previously served a six-year term for rape, attempted rape and indecent assault. Mr Baker commented:

It is a matter of regret that my learned friend used the word monster. It is my submission this man is sick…He [Pickering] claims that years of indifference to his illness, the ignoring of his pleas for treatment in prison, refusals of help in the sense of getting medical treatment, also being approached by police every time a child was attacked – all this has caused a complete mental breakdown and so led to this final sick outburst.

Mr Baker told the judge that Pickering had told him if he went to Broadmoor Hospital it would destroy him utterly and also his chances of rehabilitation. Mr Baker concluding by saying to the judge:

> *He instructs me to ask your Lordship, though he realises the chances are small, to consider a period of probation with a condition of residence for twelve months. That residence would of course be in hospital.*

Mr Justice MacKenna told Pickering:

> *I am satisfied that you are suffering from a psychopathic disorder and need very close care.*

The judge then ordered Pickering to be detained in Broadmoor. No time limitation was stipulated.

CHAPTER 16

Blame it on Poor Little Charlie, Wombwell, 2003

My husband collapsed early doors this morning. He drinks too much and I think he's had the DT's and my dogs attacked him. He's not responding to me at all and there's blood all over him... I don't know if he's breathing or dead.

By February 2003 Margaret Green, married to her husband Shaun for twenty-five years, as various newspapers remarked in their descriptions of her, was looking considerably older than her forty-six years. When I look back to 1967 when I first met the later to become Mrs Green, as far as I can tell, the abilities that she undoubtedly possessed since then had seldom been put to good use. Her quick brain and engaging personality did not see her advance very far in life. Like so many girls in her class she chose to leave school at the earliest opportunity. I hold no reservations that Margaret Crellin, as she then was, could have achieved a good position in a professional field, had she made that choice. I can personally remember Margaret when she was at Hoyland's Kirk Balk School, from the age of eleven to sixteen. She, like myself, was one of the school's first comprehensive intake. I remember Margaret being confident, mischievous, as well as a keen and not unaccomplished sportswoman. I can picture her now running apace across the field in gymslip and white knee length socks towards the girls' gym as she heard the first strains of *Band of Gold* sung by Freda Payne (at that time a particular favourite of hers) being played. Above all during that particular period, I remember her being extremely fashion conscious and, although pupils at Kirk Balk were required to wear school uniform, she would don the odd accessory and was forever dodging the beady eye of the formidable Miss Travis and later Mrs Fowlds, who were responsible for the junior and senior girls' general behaviour and conformity. During the early 1970s I remember her wearing a very fine sheepskin coat, an expensive item then, but whatever was in vogue, her parents, Sid and Doreen, saw to it that their daughter did not feel anything other than she was at the forefront of Hoyland's young female fashionable elite.

Whatever happened to that girl who showed so much promise? I moved to London in 1975 but on my frequent visits to Hoyland I remember seeing Margaret often, more than a decade later when she worked for some time at the Co-operative store on the checkout. Her personality was still as engaging as ever but her vibrancy, self-confidence and the twinkle in her eyes were no longer apparent. The strain of her mundane lifestyle was already beginning to show and her once youthful looks had degenerated into those associated with premature middle age. By the mid-1990s I no longer saw her around Hoyland and the next I heard of her was in February 2003 when I read on the front page of the *Barnsley Chronicle* in an article headlined 'Jobless woman charged with murdering husband' I learned Margaret had been charged with murdering her forty-five-year-old husband, Shaun, at their home in Wombwell.

In the early afternoon on Friday 24 February 2003, Margaret Green stabbed and slashed her alcoholic husband, Shaun, a former factory-worker, with a lock knife he used to clean his nails, while he was sitting in an armchair. At 3.00pm she phoned the emergency services. A transcript of the call was later played in court, it went:

> *My husband collapsed early doors this morning. He drinks too much and I think he's had the DT's and my dogs attacked him. He's not responding to me at all and there's blood all over him… I don't know if he's breathing or dead.*

Green later told police that on Friday 24 February, after running errands, she returned to her Loxley Avenue home in Wombwell at about noon and found her husband covered in blood. She added that he had told her that the injuries had been inflicted on him by the family dog, Charlie, a 1ft tall, ginger Lakeland Terrier. She said she had no reason to disbelieve her husband as the dog had attacked him twice before. She said the dog had become scared when his master had awoke with 'the shakes'. After she had tended to Shaun's wounds, she helped him change his clothes and had taken him to an upstairs bedroom. She also said that despite her pleas, Shaun had refused to receive medical attention. Unfortunately for Margaret Green, pathological and forensic evidence was later to show that an entirely different chain of events had taken place.

Margaret Green had become a creature of habit. Certain errands were carried out on particular days. Twice a week she delivered shopping to her wheelchair-bound, pensioner, father-in-law, Tony. She was an early riser, rarely getting up later than 6.00am. She then habitually phoned her mother. On Monday mornings she would arrive at Hough Lane Post Office at 8.55am in an attempt to beat the queues. She would then do Tony Green's shopping, deliver it and stay for a chat before returning home. On the day of the murder, having carried out her usual chores of visiting the post office and delivering Tony Green's shopping, she visited her friend Doreen Barker in Church Street, and did some more shopping before returning home to Loxley Avenue. Shortly afterwards the murderous attack on Shaun Green took place.

Exactly what prompted Margaret Green to kill her husband

The Periwinkle, *Wombwell, where in December 2002 Shaun Green was drinking with Alan Bentley.* The author may never be known, as she never admitted to the murder of which she was convicted. Following the fatal stab wound it seems most likely from the forensic evidence Green dragged her husband's, probably by then, lifeless body, upstairs to a front bedroom, where she inflicted dozens of parallel stab wounds in an attempt to imitate dog bites. Forensic tests later showed that 115 stab and slash wounds had been inflicted on Shaun Green. There were eighty-five wounds to his neck and thirty on his left arm. She then made a painstaking effort to clean up the mess. Forensic evidence showed that someone had made considerable effort in an attempt to clean bloodstains from various parts of the house. Evidence suggested that a scrubbing brush might have been used to clean up the armchair in which the victim had received the fatal wound and that attempts had been made to remove bloodstains from carpets both upstairs and downstairs. Bloodstained clothes had also been washed and there was evidence that bloodstained implements had been cleaned in the kitchen sink.

Tony Green had just consumed two bottles of wine brought to him earlier that day by his daughter-in-law, Margaret, when he learnt of his son's death. Margaret had looked after his needs for some time and on the day of her husband's death had made sure her father-in-law would not go hungry. The police weren't convinced by Margaret Green's story and she was charged with murder. When this slightly built, grey-haired woman, then aged forty-seven, appeared in the dock in September 2003 at Sheffield Crown Court the evidence was stacked against her.

Home Office Pathologist Christopher Milroy said that Shaun Green had died from a 2½ inch deep stab wound to the neck. His windpipe had been severed causing him to bleed to death. The other wounds had been so arranged as to appear that Mr Green had been bitten by their pet dog. A vet who took casts of Charlie the Lakeland Terrier's teeth concluded that the wounds found on the body of Shaun Green had not been caused by the dog at all.

Fifty-two-year-old Alan Bentley, of Richardson Walk, Wombwell, a close friend of the Greens, gave evidence in court on Monday 15 September that just before Christmas 2002 Shaun Green had been drinking with him in the Periwinkle in Wombwell. He noticed several deep scratch wounds on Shaun's neck. Mr Bentley said:

> *He told me he had recently been to the doctors because he had*
> *been having blackouts. On this occasion he had been at home*
> *and had blacked out in the kitchen. He explained that he had*
> *woken up and found Charlie at his neck and he said that was*
> *how he received the injuries.*

Mr Bentley also commented in his evidence that in over twenty
years of knowing the couple he had only witnessed one act of
violence between them. He said that more than ten years ago he
had seen Shaun punch Margaret in the face.

Prosecuting counsel, Peter Kelson, QC, said Margaret Green
had plunged the knife into her husband's neck while he sat in his
armchair in the living room. In addressing her he added:

> *When your husband was immobile you set about all those*
> *other injuries to his neck so you could blame the dog.*

While admitting to the court that she no longer believed that the
dog was responsible for her husband's fatal wounds, she
continued to deny she was in any way responsible for her
husband's murder. On Tuesday 23 September the court heard
that Shaun Green had taken to drinking after his own step-
father was murdered by his Scottish half-brother in 1997. He
would drink lager and Guiness as well as up to four litres of
cider a day.

Defending counsel, Jeremy Baker QC, told the court that
Margaret Green was a woman of good character, who had never
been in trouble before and had cared for her husband's father
for a number of years. The jury were not swayed by Mr Baker's
expostulations. Following the verdict of guilty of wilful murder,
which took the jury a little less than an hour to arrive at, after
asking the judge to consider a letter written in mitigation and
vouching for Mrs Green's good character by her cousin, Mr
Baker said:

> *The jury found by their verdict that there was no provocation*
> *before the incident took place. There certainly was a long*
> *history to this marriage and certainly it was not always a*
> *particularly happy one… A slow burn type of provocation can*
> *be taken into account as at least a partial account as to what*
> *happened…This is a case where it can be said there is no*
> *prospect of further violence. There is certainly an abundance of*
> *mitigating factors and an absence of aggravating ones.*

On Wednesday 24 September the judge, District Recorder Alan Goldsack, in passing sentence said:

> *You were convicted yesterday of murder. You have throughout denied being the killer so I do not know what caused you to kill your husband. It was a sustained attack. It included thrusting a knife deep into his neck and you then tried to make it look like the family dog was responsible. You have shown no remorse and I pass the only sentence fit in this case: life imprisonment.*

Following Margaret Green's trial and conviction Shaun Green's half-brother, Roderick McGurk, said:

> *Shaun was a great guy, a real character and this has totally shocked us. It's difficult to imagine Margaret could have done this, the marriage always seemed ok to me...I don't know what could have driven her to this. We'll never know what went on that day.*

In June 2007, Margaret Green's appeal was heard in London. Mr Justice Calvert Smith said that Green must serve at least eleven years behind bars. He said that she had behaved well in prison and accepted opportunities for self-improvement. Now aged fifty-one, Green may be released in 2014 (after time spent in remand is taken into account). When released, she will remain on perpetual licence subject to recall to prison should she offend in any way.

Sources and Further Reading

Chapter 1

The Leeds Intelligencer, Saturday December 9 1854

The Barnsley Times, Saturday June 9 1855

The Barnsley Times, Saturday July 14 1855

The Barnsley Times, Saturday March 8 1856

Barnsley Chronicle And Penistone,Wath, And Hoyland Journal,
Saturday 14 July 1860

Barnsley Chronicle And Penistone,Wath, And Hoyland Journal,
Saturday 22 September 1860

Barnsley Chronicle And Penistone,Wath, And Hoyland Journal,
Saturday February 22 1862

Barnsley Chronicle And Penistone,Wath, And Hoyland Journal,
Saturday March 1 1862

Barnsley Chronicle And Penistone,Wath, And Hoyland Journal,
Saturday July 2 1864

Barnsley Chronicle And Penistone,Wath, And Hoyland Journal,
Saturday July 9 1864

Barnsley Chronicle And Penistone,Wath, And Hoyland Journal,
Saturday December 19 1868

Barnsley Chronicle And Penistone,Wath, And Hoyland Journal,
Saturday January 2 1869 *Barnsley Chronicle And Penistone,
Wath, And Hoyland Journal,* Saturday April 3 1869

*Barnsley Standard And Wombwell Dodworth and Worsbro'
Recorder,* Saturday January 2 1892

*Barnsley Standard And Wombwell Dodworth and Worsbro'
Recorder,* Saturday January 16 1892

*Barnsley Standard And Wombwell Dodworth and Worsbro'
Recorder,* Saturday February 20 1892

*Barnsley Standard And Wombwell Dodworth and Worsbro'
Recorder,* Saturday February 27 1892

*Barnsley Chronicle And Penistone Mexbro'Wath And Hoyland
Journal,* Saturday March 23 1907

*Barnsley Chronicle And Penistone Mexbro'Wath And Hoyland
Journal,* Saturday February 8 1908

Barnsley Chronicle And Penistone Mexbro'Wath And Hoyland

Journal, Saturday April 16 1910

Barnsley Chronicle And Penistone Mexbro'Wath And Hoyland Journal, Saturday September 4 1915

Barnsley Chronicle And Penistone Mexbro'Wath And Hoyland Journal, Saturday February 15 1919

Barnsley Chronicle And Penistone Mexbro Wath And Hoyland Journal, Saturday January 28 1921

Barnsley Chronicle And Penistone Mexbro Wath And Hoyland Journal, Saturday February 5 1921

Barnsley Chronicle And Penistone Mexbro Wath And Hoyland Journal, Saturday August 20 1921

Barnsley Chronicle And Penistone Mexbro Wath And Hoyland Journal, Saturday September 9 1922

Barnsley Chronicle And Penistone Mexbro Wath And Hoyland Journal, Saturday July 4 1925

Barnsley Chronicle And Penistone Mexboro'Wath And Hoyland Journal, Saturday December 20 1930

Barnsley Chronicle And South Yorkshire News, Saturday November 29 1947

Barnsley Chronicle And South Yorkshire News, Saturday July 30 1955

Barnsley Chronicle And South Yorkshire News, Saturday April 7 1962

Barnsley Chronicle And South Yorkshire News, Saturday April 21 1962

Barnsley Chronicle, Friday 10 November 1995

Barnsley Star, Thursday November 2 1995

Barnsley Star, Tuesday November 7 1995

Barnsley Star, Wednesday November 8 1995

Chapter 2

Barnsley Chronicle And Penistone, Wath, And Hoyland Journal, Saturday April 28 1860

Barnsley Chronicle And Penistone, Wath, And Hoyland Journal, Saturday April 1 185

Barnsley Chronicle And Penistone, Wath, And Hoyland Journal, Saturday July 26 1876

Barnsley Standard And Wombwell Dodworth and Worsbro' Recorder, Saturday January 30 1892

Barnsley Chronicle And Penistone Mexboro'Wath And Hoyland Journal, Saturday January 26 1907

Barnsley Chronicle And Penistone Mexboro'Wath And Hoyland Journal, Saturday March 23 1907

Barnsley Chronicle And Penistone Mexboro'Wath And Hoyland Journal, Saturday February 15 1919

Barnsley Chronicle And Penistone Mexboro'Wath And Hoyland Journal, Saturday January 25 1930

Barnsley Chronicle And Penistone Mexboro'Wath And Hoyland Journal, Saturday June 7 1930

Barnsley Chronicle And Penistone Mexboro'Wath And Hoyland Journal, Saturday December 20 1930

Barnsley Chronicle And South Yorkshire News, Saturday December 11 1948

Barnsley Chronicle And South Yorkshire News, Saturday May 12 1951

Barnsley Chronicle, Saturday February 17 1962

Barnsley Chronicle, Friday June 23 2007

Chapter 3

Illustrated Police News, November 26 1876

Barnsley Standard And Wombwell Dodworth and Worsbro' Recorder, Saturday March 26 1892

Barnsley Chronicle And South Yorkshire News, Saturday October 25 1947

Barnsley Chronicle And South Yorkshire News, Saturday April 21 1951

Barnsley Chronicle And South Yorkshire News, Saturday May 5 1962

Barnsley Chronicle And South Yorkshire News, Saturday June 19 1965

Barnsley Chronicle, Friday September 15 1989

The Times, Friday September 15 1989

Daily Mail, Friday September 15 1989

Daily Mirror, Friday September 15 1989

Daily Express, Friday September 15 1989

The Times, Saturday September 16 1989

Barnsley Chronicle, Friday February 9 1996

Chapter 4

Barnsley Chronicle And Penistone, Wath, And Hoyland Journal, Saturday 1 April 1865

Barnsley Chronicle And Penistone, Mexbro' And Hoyland Journal, Saturday January 6 1900

Barnsley Chronicle And South Yorkshire News, Saturday July 31 1948

Chapter 5
The Leeds Intelligencer, Saturday August 19 1854
The Leeds Intelligencer, Saturday September 2 1854
The Leeds Intelligencer, Saturday December 8 1854

Chapter 6
*The Barnsley Chronicle And Penistone, Wath, And Hoyland
    Journal,* Saturday July 2 1864
*The Barnsley Chronicle And Penistone, Wath, And Hoyland
    Journal,* Saturday July 9 1864
*The Barnsley Chronicle And Penistone, Wath, And Hoyland
    Journal,* Saturday August 27 1864

Chapter 7
The Barnsley Times Saturday March 8 1856
The Barnsley Times Saturday March 22 1856

Chapter 8
*The Barnsley Chronicle And Penistone, Mexbro', Wath And
    Hoyland Journal,* Saturday April 2 1892
*The Barnsley Chronicle And Penistone, Mexbro', Wath And
    Hoyland Journal,* Saturday April 16 1892
*The Barnsley Chronicle And Penistone, Mexbro', Wath And
    Hoyland Journal,* Saturday May 28 1892
*The Barnsley Standard And Wombwell Dodworth and Worsbro'
    Recorder,* Saturday April 2 1892
*The Barnsley Standard And Wombwell Dodworth and Worsbro'
    Recorder,* Saturday April 16 1892
*The Barnsley Standard And Wombwell Dodworth and Worsbro'
    Recorder,* Saturday May 28 1892

Chapter 9
Barnsley Chronicle and South Yorkshire News, Saturday
    November 14 1942
Barnsley Chronicle and South Yorkshire News, Saturday January
    9 1943
Barnsley Chronicle and South Yorkshire News, Saturday March
    20 1943

Chapter 10
Barnsley Chronicle and South Yorkshire News, Saturday May 8
    1943
South Yorkshire Times And Express, Saturday May 8 1943

Barnsley Chronicle and South Yorkshire News, Saturday May 15
    1943
South Yorkshire Times And Express, Saturday June 5 1943
Barnsley Chronicle and South Yorkshire News, Saturday June 5
    1943
Barnsley Chronicle and South Yorkshire News, Saturday June 12
    1943
South Yorkshire Times And Express, Saturday June 12 1943
Barnsley Chronicle and South Yorkshire News, Saturday July 17
    1943
South Yorkshire Times And Express, Saturday July 17 1943
Barnsley Chronicle and South Yorkshire News, Saturday 11
    September 1943

Chapter 11
Barnsley Chronicle and South Yorkshire News, Saturday May 7
    1955
Barnsley Chronicle and South Yorkshire News, Saturday June 4
    1955
Barnsley Chronicle and South Yorkshire News, Saturday June 11
    1955
South Yorkshire Times And Express, Saturday June 11 1955
Barnsley Chronicle and South Yorkshire News, Saturday July 2
    1955
South Yorkshire Times And Express, Saturday July 2 1955
Barnsley Chronicle and South Yorkshire News, Saturday July 23
    1955
Barnsley Chronicle and South Yorkshire News, Saturday July 30
    1955
South Yorkshire Times And Express, Saturday July 30 1955
Barnsley Chronicle and South Yorkshire News, Saturday August 6
    1955
South Yorkshire Times And Express, Saturday August 6 1955
Barnsley Chronicle and South Yorkshire News, Saturday August
    13 1955

Chapter 12
Barnsley Chronicle, Saturday February 3 1962
Barnsley Chronicle, Saturday February 10 1962
Barnsley Chronicle, Saturday February 17 1962
Barnsley Chronicle, Saturday March 3 1962
Barnsley Chronicle, Saturday March 17 1962
Barnsley Chronicle, Saturday March 31 1962

Barnsley Chronicle, Friday March 9 1984
Barnsley Chronicle, Friday October 2 1992

Chapter 13
Barnsley Chronicle, Saturday February 17 1962
Barnsley Chronicle, Saturday March 10 1962
Barnsley Chronicle, Saturday April 14 1962

Chapter 14
Barnsley Chronicle and South Yorkshire News, Saturday April 21
   1962
Barnsley Chronicle and South Yorkshire News, Saturday May 12
   1962
Barnsley Chronicle and South Yorkshire News, Saturday June 2
   1962
Sheffield Star, Wednesday 30 May 1962
Yorkshire Post, Wednesday 30 May 1962

Chapter 15
The *Sun*, Saturday July 15 1972
Daily Express, Saturday July 15 1972
Morning Telegraph, Sheffield, Saturday July 15 1972
Barnsley Chronicle, Friday 21 July 1972
Barnsley Chronicle, Friday 28 July 1972
News of the World, Sunday December 10 1972
Barnsley Chronicle, Friday December 15 1972

Chapter 16
Barnsley Chronicle, Friday February 28 2003
Barnsley Chronicle, Friday September 19 2003
The Star, Wednesday September 24 2003
The Star, Thursday September 25 2003
South Yorkshire Times, Friday September 26 2003
Barnsley Chronicle, Friday September 26 2003

Index

TRUE CRIME FROM WHARNCLIFFE

Foul Deeds and Suspicious Deaths Series

Barking, Dagenham & Chadwell Heath
Barnsley
Bath
Bedford
Birmingham
Black Country
Blackburn and Hyndburn
Bolton
Bradford
Brighton
Bristol
Cambridge
Carlisle
Chesterfield
Colchester
Coventry
Croydon
Derby
Durham
Ealing
Folkestone and Dover
Grimsby
Guernsey
Guilford
Halifax
Hampstead, Holborn and St Pancras
Huddersfield
Hull

Leeds
Leicester
Lewisham and Deptford
Liverpool
London's East End
London's West End
Manchester
Mansfield
More Foul Deeds Birmingham
More Foul Deeds Chesterfield
More Foul Deeds Wakefield
Newcastle
Newport
Norfolk
Northampton
Nottingham
Oxfordshire
Pontefract and Castleford
Portsmouth
Rotherham
Scunthorpe
Southend-on-Sea
Staffordshire and The Potteries
Stratford and South Warwickshire
Tees
Warwickshire
Wigan
York

OTHER TRUE CRIME BOOKS FROM WHARNCLIFFE

A-Z Yorkshire Murder
Black Barnsley
Brighton Crime and Vice 1800-2000
Durham Executions
Essex Murders
Executions & Hangings in Newcastle
   and Morpeth
Norfolk Mayhem and Murder

Norwich Murders
Strangeways Hanged
The A-Z of London Murders
Unsolved Murders in Victorian and
   Edwardian London
Unsolved Norfolk Murders
Unsolved Yorkshire Murders
Yorkshire's Murderous Women

Please contact us via any of the methods below for more information or a catalogue.

WHARNCLIFFE BOOKS

47 Church Street – Barnsley – South Yorkshire – S70 2AS
Tel: 01226 734555 – 734222 Fax: 01226 – 734438
E-mail: enquiries@pen-and-sword.co.uk
Website: www.wharncliffebooks.co.uk